HOW
—— *to* ——
CONTINUE
—— *the* ——
CHRISTIAN
—— *life* ——

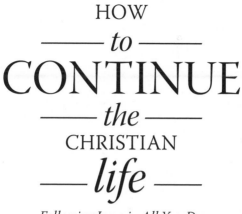

HOW
to
CONTINUE
the
CHRISTIAN
life

Following Jesus in All You Do

GEORGE SWEETING

MOODY PUBLISHERS
CHICAGO

All Scripture quotations, unless otherwise indicated, are taken from the *New King James Version*. Copyright © 1982 by Thomas Nelson, Inc. Used by permission. All rights reserved.

Scripture quotations marked NASB are taken from the *New American Standard Bible*®, Copyright © 1960, 1962, 1963, 1968, 1971, 1972, 1973, 1975, 1977, and 1995 by The Lockman Foundation, La Habra, Calif. Used by permission.

Scripture quotations marked NIV are taken from the *Holy Bible: New International Version*®. NIV®. Copyright © 1973, 1978, 1984 by Biblica, Inc.™ Used by permission of Zondervan. All rights reserved worldwide. www.zondervan.com.

Scripture quotations marked KJV are taken from the King James Version.

Scripture quotations marked WILLIAMS are taken from *The New Testament in the Language of the People*, Charles B. Williams, translator. Copyright © 1937, 1965 by Bruce Humphries; renewed 1965; © 1966 by Edith S. Williams. Used by permission of Moody Publishers.

Edited by Jim Vincent
Interior design: Ragont Design
Cover design: Kathryn Duckett
Cover illustration: Hypergon, Inc. / 2007 iStock

Library of Congress Cataloging-in-Publication Data

Sweeting, George, 1924-
  How to continue the Christian life / George Sweeting.
    p. cm.
  Includes bibliographical references.
  ISBN 978-0-8024-3601-6
  1. Christian life. 2. Spiritual formation. I. Title.
  BV4501.3.S9445 2013
  248.4--dc23
                        2012035358

We hope you enjoy this book from Moody Publishers. Our goal is to provide high-quality, thought-provoking books and products that connect truth to your real needs and challenges. For more information on other books and products written and produced from a biblical perspective, go to www.moodypublishers.com or write to:

Moody Publishers
820 N. LaSalle Boulevard
Chicago, IL 60610

1 3 5 7 9 10 8 6 4 2

Printed in the United States of America

To my best earthly friend and partner in marriage:
Margaret Hilda Sweeting

CONTENTS

A Personal Note   9
Appreciation   11

1. God's Awesome Work of Salvation   13

2. The Call to Follow Jesus   25

3. Worshiping God in Spirit and in Truth   41

4. Prayer and Fasting   59

5. Going Deeper into the Word of God   83

6. The Role of the Holy Spirit in   101
    Christian Growth

7. How to Become a Love-Filled Person   113

8. Loving One Another through the   127
    Church and Spiritual Gifts

9. Christian Service and the Christian's Work   141

10. A Generous Impulse   165

11. How to Know the Will of God   181

12. Sharing the Good News   207

A PERSONAL NOTE

MY DEAR FRIEND,

As I sit at my desk, I want to write a personal note to each reader about why I've written this book.

As I have served as a pastor and a college president, I've observed a serious condition among Christians in general. There appears to be a startling disparity between what Christians *profess* and what they *do* in their daily lives. Although they claim the Bible as their authority, they appear oblivious to its call.

The call of the Bible is for each follower of Christ "to be conformed to the image of [God's] Son" (Romans 8:29). To miss this call is to miss the Christian life.

A giant delusion exists that only a certain few are called to experience a life of victory. In reality, the Bible calls each Christian to "continue to live . . . in Him, rooted and built up in Him" (Colossians 2:6–7 NIV).

On a personal level, I would lovingly urge you to "continue in the things which you have learned" (2 Timothy 3:14).

Success in the Christian life depends on our choices, not good intentions. Warmly, I encourage you to *continue* the good work of salvation that God has begun.

George Sweeting
ROMANS 6:22

APPRECIATION

MY FIRST BOOK, *How to Begin the Christian Life*, has been in print since 1975. Since then, it has sold over one million copies and has been translated into more than one dozen languages.

Because of the urging of new believers and fellow pastors, I wrote this sequel, *How to Continue the Christian Life*, in 1998. This is the first revision of the title.

I owe a special debt of gratitude to my son, Dr. Don Sweeting, who persistently urged me to "just do it."

Also, I am grateful to my granddaughter, Erica Sweeting Dawson, for typing this manuscript. Lastly, I want to thank Jim Vincent of Moody Publishers for his wise and caring editing of this manuscript.

"As you received Christ Jesus as Lord,
continue to live in him."

Colossians 2:6 (NIV, italics added)

"God's awesome work of salvation is our primary
motivation to continue the Christian life."

George Sweeting

"If anyone is in Christ, he is a new creation;
old things have passed away;
behold, all things have become new."

2 Corinthians 5:17

"You have made us for Yourself, O Lord,
and our heart is restless until it finds rest in You."

Augustine, *Confessions*

1

GOD'S AWESOME WORK OF SALVATION

EIGHT HUNDRED YEARS AGO, Europe witnessed a startling event. In 1212, the spirit of the Crusades charmed a young French boy named Stephen, who took up a cross and started marching. Soon, thousands of children, tired of tending sheep and working on the farms, began to follow him. Stephen promised to lead them over the mountains and through the seas "to God." Eventually they would march past Tours and Lyons to Marseilles and seek passage by ship to Palestine.[1]

Meanwhile, in Germany a slightly older boy, Nicholas, gathered an army of children and entered Switzerland, marching through Geneva and soon crossing the Alps. Carrying their wooden crosses, they sang while they marched down the hills and valleys of Italy. Finally they reached Genoa, Italy.[2] They came—by the thousands—with but one chorus on their lips, "We are going to God."

Historians believe that the real reason for the Children's Crusade was that these young people wanted to escape the emptiness of everyday life. Possibly this is why so many children were inspired by the calls of Stephen and Nicholas to adventure.

But did they escape? The answer is *no*! When they came to Genoa and Venice, they met every kind of evil. Some of the German children took a ship to Palestine but were never heard from again. Others accompanied Nicholas to Rome and met with the pope, who advised them to return home and fight for the cross when they grew up. During their return, most could not endure the journey, so they settled in Italian villages, never to see their parents again. Only a few stragglers were able to recross the Alps and return to Germany.

The French children under Stephen fared worse. Promising to deliver them to Palestine, slave traders carried some to Bougie on the Algerian coast, where they sold the children into a life of bondage. Others were taken by ship to Baghdad and told to accept Islam or die. Still others were taken to Egypt, where they served a governor in captivity.[3]

Some became ill and died, others were robbed and molested. Most turned back, without a cross . . . and without a song.

PEOPLE WANT A NEW START

The children had wanted a purpose for their ordinary lives. Today people still want purpose for their lives. During one foggy night at O'Hare International Airport, only a few planes were able to depart from Chicago. One jet raced down the runway and quickly disappeared into the fog. A wife watching in a terminal whispered to her husband, "I wish I could escape just like that plane, and have a new start . . . somewhere else!"

The wife was apparently successful, yet she felt unfulfilled. Why did she want to escape . . . and start over? Because like most of us, she found life incomplete intellectually, morally, and spiritually. All of us know what is right and good, yet on every side we experience what is wrong and evil. Daily we're confronted with corruption in government, dishonesty in business, and cheating in marriage. Our faith in others and even in ourselves is often shattered.

LIFE ON THE NATURAL
PLANE IS INCOMPLETE

One way or another, our words and actions announce how incomplete we really are. Life is like a big hole, waiting and wanting to be filled. From day to day, we pour an astonishing collection of things into that hole: work projects, television, sports, travel, volunteer service, study, and parties, and yet if we're honest, all our efforts leave us unfulfilled and longing for something more.

Blaise Pascal, mathematician and physicist, said, "There's a God-shaped vacuum in every life." It is my firm belief that *only God* can fill that God-shaped vacuum!

We were created for friendship and partnership with God. However, our original relationship with God was broken by human disobedience and sin.

The Old Testament prophet Isaiah expresses our condition with these words, "All we like sheep have gone astray; we have turned, every one, to his own way" (Isaiah 53:6). Our primary need is to acknowledge our sinfulness and turn to God, asking forgiveness and restoration. The gospel of John reads, "As many as received Him, to them He gave the right to become children of God, to those who believe in His name" (John 1:12).

As we will see shortly, receiving Jesus as Savior and Lord is the first step to completeness.

LIFE ON THE NATURAL
PLANE IS DISAPPOINTING

Little in life measures up to our expectations.

William Saroyan, in his classic play *The Human Comedy*, graphically illustrates the disappointment of life on the natural plane. Saroyan introduces us to an immigrant father, Mr. Ara, and his three-year-old boy, John, in their produce store in Ithaca, California. The son asks his father for an apple, but after the boy is granted this request and has eaten the apple, it fails to make him happy. The son then asks for an orange, but this too results in disappointment. "Give me candy," asks the boy. The father selected the most popular bar of candy, only to discover that his boy was disappointed, finding the candy to be "nothing, truly nothing."

After repeating this search with a variety of things, the exasperated father looks at his boy and says, "You want apple. I give you apple. You want orange. I give you orange. You want candy. I give you candy. You want banana. I give you banana. What you want now?"

Then, speaking to his son, but at the same time speaking to everyone, worldwide, Ara confesses, "Everybody wants things . . . Nobody knows what he wants. He just want. He look at God and say, 'Give me dis. Give me dat'—but he never satisfied. Always he want. Always he feel bad."[4]

In our heart of hearts, we too are disappointed and forced to admit that *nothing* measures up to life's expectations, because we are panting creatures who are made for so much more.

LIFE ON THE NATURAL
PLANE IS SINFUL

Seldom have I had to convince anyone of their sinfulness. Though some people have sinned more than others, all humans *have sinned.* Most people agree with the Bible verse found in Romans chapter three: "All have sinned and fall short of the glory of God" (verse 23) God's standard is perfection and all fall short of that.

Romans 3:9–20 clearly remind us that life on the natural plane is sinful.

LIFE ON THE NATURAL
PLANE CAN BE CHANGED!

There is an answer to our incompleteness and sin. A new start is possible! The apostle Paul says it this way: "If anyone is in Christ, he is a new creation; old things have passed away; behold, all things have become new" (2 Corinthians 5:17). So receiving Jesus as Savior and Lord is the first step to completeness.

This new start that Paul speaks of is not necessarily found in a new geographic location. It's natural to look for another place for a new start. Historically, groups and individuals have moved to other locations seeking a new beginning, only to find that sin is everywhere because the individual is the problem.

I know a woman who continually moves, seeking one job after another simply because she can't get along with her parents. However, it is not a new job or even a new location that will provide a new start.

The chance for a new start is found in experiencing God's awesome salvation! Jesus said to Nicodemus, "Most assuredly, I say to you, unless one is *born again*, he cannot see the kingdom of God" (John 3:3, emphasis added).

If you are unsure of your salvation, this is a good

time to examine your life and make sure that you are included in God's great family. God's awesome work of salvation is the primary reason to continue the Christian life.

HAVE YOU HAD A SPIRITUAL BIRTH?

Several years ago, I was invited to speak at the National Religious Broadcasters Convention in Washington, DC. Members of the Senate and House of Representatives are invited each year to a banquet as guests of this organization. On that occasion, I had the honor of sitting next to President Jimmy Carter and former president Gerald Ford.

As we conversed during the dinner, we discovered that President Carter and I were born on the *same day and same year*: October 1, 1924. We enjoyed sharing about the 1920s and the 1930s.

Somewhere in our conversation, we both talked about *another* birthday . . . our *spiritual* birthday.

We shared how by a decision of faith, we individually, though in different geographic locations, confessed our need to God in prayer and invited Jesus to be our Lord and Savior. The president made his decision in Plains, Georgia, and I in Hawthorne, New

Jersey. That sincere decision marked our spiritual birthday.

Jesus said that without this spiritual birth we cannot "see the kingdom of God" (John 3:3).

The apostle Paul, writing to the followers of Jesus in the city of Rome, spoke of a spiritual birth with these words. "If you *confess* with your mouth, 'Jesus is Lord,' and *believe* in your heart that God raised him from the dead, *you will be saved*" (Romans 10:9 NIV, emphasis added).

God's salvation is available! You can be changed! Romans 6:23 reminds us that "the wages of sin is death, but the gift of God is eternal life *in Christ Jesus our Lord.*"

TIME FOR A NEW START

I began this chapter by telling of a woman at O'Hare International Airport who was prepared by God to experience God's great salvation. I had the joyful privilege of sharing the gospel with her and her husband.

From the Scriptures, I explained that each person is spiritually dead in trespasses and sins and, therefore, helpless and incapable of saving himself. I also shared that only God could intervene to save us because we are by birth, by nature, and by choice in bondage to self and sin. Something had to be done *in us* and *for us* before we could become a child of God.

I then told them how Jesus, on the cross, freely became our sin bearer, so that we might experience God's salvation. "All this is from God, who reconciled us to himself through Christ" (2 Corinthians 5:18 NIV).

Amid the distractions of the airport, they seriously, yet simply, asked God in prayer to give them a new start, a spiritual start. For them and for me it was a life-changing experience.

OUR RIGHT RESPONSE
TO GOD'S LOVE

When a follower of Jesus understands, even in a limited way, God's great love; when we catch a glimpse of God's holiness; when we understand, even in a measure, God's condescension to visit earth in human form at Bethlehem; when we realize the willingness of Jesus to bear our sins in His body on the cross; when we enter, even to a small degree, into His sufferings for our sins—*then* our only reasonable response is to give ourselves to Him so that His purpose will be fulfilled, which the Bible says is: "to be conformed to the image of His Son" (Romans 8:29).

This is God's plan for you and me. To miss this is to *miss the Christian life.*

God's *awesome work of salvation* is our primary reason . . . to continue the Christian life.

QUESTIONS

1. Why does everyone need a new beginning?
2. Suggest several verses of Scripture that call for a new beginning.
3. Give several reasons for the logic of continuing the Christian life.
4. Discuss several of the works of God in salvation.

NOTES

1. An estimated 30,000 children followed Stephen during his initial march through France. Nicholas of Germany would attract more than 20,000 children. See "The Children's Crusade," History Learning Site, at www. history learningsite.co.uk/childrens_crusade.htm.
2. "The Children's Crusades (1212)" *The History Guide: Lectures on Ancient and Medieval European History*, Lecture 25: The Holy Crusades; at www.historyguide. org/ancient/children.html.
3. Ibid.
4. William Saroyan, *The Human Comedy* (New York: Harcourt, Brace, 1943, 1971), 125.

"Just as you received Christ Jesus as Lord, continue to live in him, rooted and built up in him, strengthened in the faith as you were taught."

Colossians 2:6–7 (NIV)

"Millions of people in our culture make decisions for Christ, but there is a dreadful attrition rate. . . . In our kind of culture anything, even news about God, can be sold if it is packaged freshly; but when it loses its novelty, it goes in the garbage heap. There is a great market for the religious experience in our world; there is little enthusiasm for the patient acquisition of virtue, little inclination to sign up for a long apprenticeship."

Eugene Peterson
A Long Obedience in the Same Direction

"Follow my example, as I follow the example of Christ."

1 Corinthians 11:1 (NIV)

2

THE CALL TO FOLLOW JESUS

WHEN A PERSON DIES, often someone will ask, "How much was he worth?" followed by an answer in dollars and cents. However, that's false! In reality, I am worth no more than the measure of growth in becoming like Jesus. Even though salvation is awesome, it is *just the beginning* of God's plan for us!

When Jesus called to the twelve disciples, He simply said, "Follow Me."

"Follow Me, and I will make you fishers of men," He said. Immediately they followed Jesus (see Matthew 4:19–20). It was the same in the gospel of John; after Jesus called them, they followed Him (John 1:37, 43).

Continuing the Christian life means to follow Jesus day after day. It means increasingly being conformed to the likeness of Jesus (Romans 8:29). It means to be holy.

The apostle Paul charged the believers in the Greek city of Corinth, "Follow my example, as I follow the example of Christ" (1 Corinthians 11:1 NIV).

It is important to ask, "Am I following Jesus?" "Am I more interested in the things of God today than I was last year?"

There's a mega delusion among Christians that only a select few are called to live Christlike lives! To the contrary, Ephesians 1:4 calls *all* believers to live "holy and without blame before Him in love."

OUR PURPOSE IN CHRIST: BE HOLY

The world in which we live calls us to live for self, gratification, and fame, but God calls us to live a holy life through Christ. Paul reminded the followers of Jesus in the city of Ephesus that they were chosen by God "before the foundation of the world" for this number one purpose of being holy (Ephesians 1:4).

So what is holiness? Holiness is the joyful experience of God's character rubbing off on my character, by the faithful work of the Holy Spirit.

"Holiness," observed Charles Colson, "is not the private preserve of an elite corps of martyrs, mystics and Nobel Prize winners." To the contrary, holiness is everyday living for everyday people, under the leadership of the Holy Spirit.

HOLINESS IS A GIFT: SALVATION

Holiness begins with God. In his vision of heaven, the prophet Isaiah heard the angels calling, "Holy, holy, holy is the Lord of hosts" (Isaiah 6:3).

When used with reference to God, holiness speaks of God's self-sufficiency. He is independent of all other created things. Holiness also refers to the infinite perfection of all God's attributes. However, the most frequent references to God's holiness speak of His moral excellence. The prophet announces, "You are of purer eyes than to behold evil, and cannot look on wickedness" (Habakkuk 1:13).

But God is holy and we are unholy. God is righteous (Romans 3:21) and we're unrighteous. Scripture declares, "All have sinned and fall short of the glory of God" (3:23). A huge gap separates the holy God of verse 21 from the sinful man of verse 23. In the middle stands the righteous God-man, Jesus Christ. The righteousness of God comes to people like you and me, *in only one way*—through faith in Jesus Christ. Justification, which simply means a right standing with God, is a *gift* of God's grace. We receive it through faith in the saving work of Christ on the cross (3:24; 5:1).

But, how is the gift of God's holiness *applied* to you and me?

First of all, holiness is *pictured* for us in history by the obedient life of Jesus. He was the sinless Son who fully obeyed the Father's will to the point of dying on the cross.

Second, holiness is *established* in history because death could not *hold* Jesus, the obedient servant. Death was defeated. Jesus broke the hold of death by His resurrection (1 Corinthians 15:20–21).

Third, holiness is *transferred* in history from Christ to you and to me. Jesus Christ died in my place. He became my Savior-substitute. He took the penalty for my sin upon Himself—the penalty I deserved and He did not deserve.

That's why Christians say, "Christ died for our sins" (1 Corinthians 15:3). By His death, He saved us from eternal death and removed our guilt before God. So we are not only redeemed, but are made victorious and are reconciled to God. In a wonderful, awesome exchange, Christ took away our sin and gave us His righteousness, so that sinners may freely come to

God through Jesus, clothed in His holy character.

Fourth, holiness is *applied* in history when God sees those who believe in Jesus Christ, and pronounces them justified. By faith, we become holy. By faith we become saints. Because our sins have been dealt with, we have a right standing with God.

Always remember that holiness is a gift from God. By faith alone, we became new creatures in Christ. By faith, we have a new identity. By faith, we are crucified and resurrected with Christ. By faith, we emerge from the cocoon of sin and death to God's righteousness and eternal life. Holiness is a gift from God to all who receive Jesus as Lord and Savior.

HOLINESS IS A COMMAND: SANCTIFICATION

God commands us to be holy. "But as He who called you is holy, you also be holy in all your conduct, because it is written, 'Be holy, for I am holy'" (1 Peter 1:15–16). This is God's call to *continue* working out the implications of receiving Jesus as Lord and Savior. If conversion is real, it *automatically* leads to a desire for a new pattern of living.

From God's view, a new beginning takes place when we receive Christ. This beginning, or rebirth, is called *regeneration*. God awakens our spirit and gives us His divine life. God turns on the generator of faith and enables us to believe. From man's view, the change is *conversion*. We take a new direction in life with a new reference point. Instead of living for self and things, we now desire to live for Jesus Christ.

But this is merely the beginning of change. If our conversion is real, it needs to be followed by the daily, continued *living out* of our new identity. This experience is called *sanctification.*

Don't be afraid of this word. The word *sanctification* simply means "to set apart." It has the same root as the words *saint* and *holy*. In general, it means to dedicate ourselves wholly to God, for His use (Psalm 4:3). Sanctification and holiness are much the same.

The moment a person receives Jesus Christ as Savior, he is sanctified. We refer to this as *initial* sanctification. The same act of faith that brings us into God's family also brings us *positional* sanctification, or *justification*, in which God declares us holy. Hebrews 10:10 says, "We have been sanctified through the offering of the body of Jesus Christ once for all."

This positional sanctification is ours because we have been born into God's family by faith in Christ, regardless of our degree of spirituality. That's why Paul could say to the Corinthian believers, in spite of their carnal ways, "And such were some of you. But you were washed, but you were sanctified, but you were justified in the name of the Lord Jesus and by the Spirit of our God" (1 Corinthians 6:11). God sets all believers apart for Himself positionally the very moment they receive Him as Lord and Savior.

But there's more. Sanctification continues for the believer's earthly lifetime. This is sometimes called *progressive* sanctification. It speaks of a daily recognition and submission to Jesus as our Sovereign Lord, of becoming holy, so that our daily living matches our new standing with God.

Before receiving Jesus as Savior, we were slaves to sin and self (Romans 6:20). In reality, we were hostile to God and controlled by our sinful desires. But the apostle Paul tells us of a marvelous transformation: "But now having been set free from sin, and having become slaves of God, you have your fruit to holiness, and the end, everlasting life" (Romans 6:22).

Instead of being slaves to sin, we are now the sons and we choose to be "slaves of God." On a daily basis, we can enjoy the fruit of holiness (Romans 6:22); the fruit of the Spirit, such as love, joy, and peace (see Galatians 5:22–23); and the abundant life (John 10:10).

Because of God's call to a holy life, we, as believers, are wholeheartedly *for* all that God is for, and *against* all that God is against.

Our sanctification will be completed at the coming of Jesus Christ. Then we will be like Jesus and enjoy complete sanctification of body, soul, and spirit (see 1 Thessalonians 5:23; also 3:12–13; Philippians 3:20–21).

Colossians 1:21–23 forcefully reminds us of God's command: "And you, who once were alienated and enemies in your mind by wicked works, yet now He has reconciled in the body of His flesh through death." Why? "To present you holy, and blameless, and above reproach in His sight." The verse continues: "If indeed you continue in the faith." The call to be a Christian is the identical call to live a holy life.

HOLINESS IS A PROCESS

Justification and sanctification have similarities. Both are part of God's great work of salvation provided by Christ. Both are available because of God's mercy and grace. Both begin at the same time. But they refer to different phases of our new life in Christ.

Justification is the act where *God declares sinners righteous*. It is based on Christ's righteousness. Sanctification is the *ongoing process* of becoming holy in practice and is brought about by the work of the Holy Spirit. In justification, works play no part at all. In sanctification, works are important. Justification is a perfect, complete act. Sanctification is a progressive process. Justification gives us a title to heaven, but sanctification actually prepares us for heaven.

A holy life will mirror the characteristics of Galatians 5:22. We would do well to examine ourselves and see if the elements of the fruit of the Spirit are traits exhibited in our daily lives. Am I a love-filled person? Do I reflect authentic joy? Does God's peace reign in my life? Am I patient and steadfast? Am I gentle?

Likewise, James 3:17 lists the qualities of heavenly wisdom. I need to ask: Is my life pure? Am I peaceable? Philippians 4:8 suggests the marks of a transformed mind. Are these character traits seen in my life? First Corinthians 13:4–5 describes the characteristics of divine love, as well as the character traits of Jesus Christ. Each of us needs to ask: Are those traits my traits?

The point of sanctification is to grow in the holiness we have received. A life of no growth for the Christian is pathetic—just as a baby who doesn't grow is a tragedy.

Ask the average college freshman if he wants to remain a freshman forever. The thought is horrifying to him. Freshmen live to be upperclassmen, just as believers live to become like Jesus.

Some people seem to think of holiness as anemic. One look at Jesus should correct that idea. The holiness of Jesus was not a sticky, stuffy, stick-your-head-in-the-sand super-spirituality. Not at all! It was a rugged, robust, realistic, right-minded resolve. Its purpose was not to keep us *from* the world, but to drive us *into* the world for God's glory.

As Leonard Ravenhill said, "God takes unholy people out of an unholy world and makes them holy, and then puts them back into that unholy world, and keeps them there."[1]

Neither should we think of holiness as an instantaneous leap that simply requires a passive letting go and letting God. At times, the Holy Spirit may work through special visitations. But that is not the normal pattern of the New Testament. The normal pattern is that the Holy Spirit indwells us when we confess Christ as Lord and Savior. From then on, the point is not that we have more of the Spirit, *but that the Holy Spirit has more of us.*

HOLINESS IS A BATTLE

Listen carefully, dear friend. Growing in holiness is a battle. It requires more than passivity. Paul describes the Christian life as all-out war. He told Timothy to "fight the good fight" (1 Timothy 6:12). We are to overcome the world, the flesh, and the Devil.

Sometimes we fail miserably. Paul did. Read Romans 7–8. Paul admits, as a seasoned apostle, "For I know that in me (that is, in my flesh) nothing good dwells; for to will is present with me, but how to perform what is good I do not find" (7:18).

How did Paul respond to failure? He did not wallow in defeat, for he knew there was no condemnation to those in Christ (8:1). He knew that the Spirit was at work in him (8:11), and that God was enthusiastically *for him* (8:31).

HOLINESS MEANS
WE TRUST AND OBEY GOD

Paul's strategy for holy living was twofold. It can be seen throughout his writings, but Philippians 2:12–13 best sums it up. There, he wrote, "Work out your own salvation with fear and trembling; for it is God who works in you both to will and to do for His good pleasure."

Paul commends both *working* and *waiting*. He trusts in the God who is at work inside him. This, in turn, prompts him to obey God's commands and work out his salvation.

What must we do to grow in holiness? Two simple things. First, like Paul, *we trust*. God is at work in us. His only Son stands ready to help us as our Prophet, Priest, and King. His Holy Spirit helps us. We rely on God's power to make the difference in our battles. We are not self-reliant. Nevertheless, we are not inactive. Trust is active.

There's a second thing we can do to grow in holiness. *We obey*. We work out our own salvation. We watch, fight, pray, draw near to God, resist the Devil, obey God's law, and put to death the deeds of the flesh. We're vigilant and resolutely obedient.

I like what Richard Owen Roberts recommends: "Each day I come to grips with the fact that I have been elected to be holy, that I am indeed in Christ, dead to sin. Each day I must refuse to give place to the old man who is dead, and every day I must in faith allow the new man to live for Christ. This day-by-day reckoning is the key to holiness."[2]

To be justified before God we need *only believe.* Faith alone is all that's necessary. To be sanctified, however, we must *trust and obey.* As the gospel song suggests, there is "no other way to be happy in Jesus." And, I might add, there is also no other way to be "holy in Jesus."

HOLINESS IS A PROMISE

Christian perfection is not possible in this life. Yet, just because it is not possible does not mean it's not relevant. Though we are not sinless, we ought to sin less and less and less. Holiness is a gift. It is a command. Holiness is also a promise.

For the believer, this life is preparation for heaven. Residence in heaven will far outlast our short life on earth. Therefore, it's not wrong to see the Christian life on earth as a prep course, and a very short one at that.

Someday, God's holiness will rule. God will sweep the universe clean and create a new heaven and a new earth—an earth that is morally just. The wicked will be judged, and the righteous will be vindicated. Peter says, "Nevertheless we, according to His promise, look for new heavens and a new earth in which righteousness dwells" (2 Peter 3:13). *Holiness has an immense future. It's worth your TOTAL investment!*

Not only are we assured that God's holy enterprise has eternal promise, we have God's assurance that His work of holiness has an eternal future. When His gift has been received by good soil, when it has grown through regular sunlight and cultivation, we can be assured of a giant future harvest.

What does God promise? God promises to continue the work He has started: "He who has begun a good work in you will *complete it* until the day of Jesus Christ" (Philippians 1:6, italics added). Paul assured the Roman believers that "whom He foreknew, He also predestined to be conformed to the image of His Son" (Romans 8:29).

Paul's point is that God continues what He starts. God is not a quitter. He will finish His special work. The game isn't over 'til it's over!

God has called us to be holy, and He has provided *the power* to make it possible. Our responsibility is to appropriate that power.

God's salvation is awesome! It's a gift. Have you received it? It's a command. Will you obey it? It's a promise. Will you appropriate it? It's for you and me, NOW!

QUESTIONS

1. Why is holiness not optional? Suggest several passages that affirm this.
2. Define the words *justification* and *sanctification*.
3. How does sanctification apply to everyday living?
4. What is Paul saying in Philippians 2:12–13?
5. What is the Christian's future regarding holiness?

NOTES

1. Leonard Ravenhill in *Draper's Book of Quotations for the Christian World*, comp. Edythe Draper (Wheaton: Tyndale, 1992), 312.
2. Richard Owen Roberts, "The Power for Holiness," *Practical Christianity* (Wheaton: Tyndale, 1987), 72.

"They were continually devoting themselves
to the apostles' teaching and to fellowship,
to the breaking of bread and to prayer."

ACTS 2:42 (NASB)

"To great sections of the church, the art of worship
has been lost entirely, and in its place has come that
strange and foreign thing called the 'program.' This
word has been borrowed from the stage and applied
with sad wisdom to the type of public service which
now passes for worship among us."

A. W. TOZER, *THE PURSUIT OF GOD*

"You are worthy, O Lord, to receive glory and honor
and power; for You have created all things, and by
Your will they exist and were created."

REVELATION 4:11

"The Christian's instincts of trust and worship are
stimulated very powerfully by knowledge of the
greatness of God. But this is knowledge that
Christians today largely lack: and that is one reason
why our faith is so feeble and our worship so flabby.
We are modern people, and modern people, though
they cherish great thoughts of themselves,
have as a rule small thoughts of God."

J. I. PACKER, *KNOWING GOD*

3

WORSHIPING GOD IN SPIRIT AND IN TRUTH

OF ALL OUR RESPONSES to the triune God, *worship*, along with faith and love, rule supreme. Worship is God's way for you and me to continue the Christian life.

Angels and men *exist* to worship God. John the apostle reminds us that the angels "do not rest day or night, saying: 'Holy, holy, holy, Lord God Almighty, who was and is and is to come!'" (Revelation 4:8).

We are also told that these "living creatures give glory and honor and thanks to Him who sits on the throne, . . . [casting] their crowns before the throne, saying: 'You are worthy, O Lord, to receive glory and honor and power'" (Revelation 4:9–11).

Jesus Himself told us about the kind of people God wants to worship Him: "But the hour is coming, and now is, when the true worshipers will worship the

Father *in spirit and truth*; for the Father is seeking such to worship Him" (John 4:23; italics added).

The Samaritan woman thought that worship was tied to a geographical place. After all, the Samaritans claimed that true worship took place in *their* country, in *their* temple, on *their* Mount Gerizim. The Jews countered that Jerusalem was the primary place of worship.

Jesus' concern in John 4 was to show the woman of Samaria, and all others who limit worship to a time and place, that God is not bound to a location. He is truth, and He is spirit. Therefore, He can be sought and found anywhere. In other words, worship can't be confined to the corners of our lives, but should fill all we do with glory and divine meaning.

WHAT IS WORSHIP?

So what is worship? Like many great words of the Bible, *worship* is difficult to define. Someone has defined worship as "the overflow of a grateful heart under the sense of God's favor," much like David, as he sang, "My heart is overflowing with a good theme" (Psalm 45:1). As David thought about the glory and goodness of God, his soul bubbled over in gratitude.

Another definition for worship is "the occupation

of the heart, not with its needs or blessings, but with God Himself." Second Samuel 7:18–22 illustrates this, closing with the statement, "You are great, O Lord God. For there is none like You, nor is there any God besides You" (v. 22). The Lord God was David's life.

Pastor and author Warren Wiersbe has this to say about worship:

> When you consider all of the words used for worship in both the Old and New Testaments, and when you put the meanings together, you find that worship involves both attitudes (awe, reverence, respect) and actions (bowing, praising, serving). It is both a subjective experience and an objective activity. Worship is not an unexpressed feeling, nor is it an empty formality. True worship is balanced and involves the mind, the emotions, and the will. It must be intelligent; it must reach deep within and be motivated by love; it must lead to obedient actions that glorify God.[1]

Worship is not listening to great preaching or even enjoying great singing and certainly not a performance. It isn't even inspired praying. It is fellowship with God Himself. It is the communion of our soul with God.

The word *worship* comes from the Old English word *worthship*. It means "to ascribe worth." The main Old Testament word for *worship* means "to bow down." The Israelite approached the holy presence of God prostrate, with holy reverence. The main New Testament word for worship means literally "to kiss toward." It speaks of submissive lowliness and deep respect. When an Israelite worshiped God, he or she ascribed supreme worth to Him. Their God alone was worthy. Why? Because God created and redeemed the people of Israel. He entered into a covenant with Israel.

But we're not Israel. Are we, then, excluded from worshiping God? Surely not. Yes, we were outside the covenant. We were estranged from God and His promises. We were dead to God in our sins. But, by God's grace, we are redeemed from sin's curse through Jesus Christ. He is our Savior, and through Him we are able to offer worship to God.

As believers in Jesus Christ, we are members of His body, the church, and are called to be a worshiping community, like Israel. First Peter 2:9–10 reminds us: "You are a chosen generation, a royal priesthood, a holy nation, His own special people, that you may proclaim the praises of Him who called you out of darkness into His marvelous light; who once were not a people but are now the people of God."

As the church, then, we come to God the Father through the person of God the Son, by the help of God the Holy Spirit. This coming to God means offering ourselves to God. It means rubbing our cold, tired, soiled lives against the beauty of His holiness.

As William Temple wrote,

> To worship is to *quicken the conscience* by the holiness of God,
> To *feed the mind* by the truth of God,
> To *purge the imagination* by the beauty of God,
> To *open the heart* by the love of God,
> And to *devote the will* to the purpose of God.

When we worship, we put our hurried lives into eternal perspective. We see that God is great and we are small. We're humbled, and this fresh dose of humility is medicine to our souls. Perhaps that's why Thomas Carlyle said, "No greater calamity can befall a nation than the loss of worship."

When we lose worship, we lose humility. And when we lose humility, we deceive ourselves and set ourselves up for a gigantic fall.

WORSHIP AS ATTITUDE
AND AS ACTION

As Jesus emphasized to the woman of Samaria, worship is not only an *act* but an *attitude.* This truth is often lost in the more formal churches. Members are tempted to think of worship exclusively as an act. Worship is confined to a liturgy or a service or a day or a season. They have forgotten that true worshipers worship God in spirit and truth. In other words, worship should reach into all the areas of our lives. The apostle Paul reminds us, "Therefore, whether you eat or drink, or whatever you do, *do all* to the glory of God" (1 Corinthians 10:31, italics added). The ideal is to live in continual openness to our Lord. It is to accent our words and deeds with inward praise to God.

Yet the *act* of worship remains very important. This may be what A. W. Tozer meant when he spoke of worship as "the missing jewel."[2] We have lost the act of worship. Even President Theodore Roosevelt reminded us, "You may worship God anywhere, at any time, but the chances are that you will not do so unless you have first learned to worship Him in some particular place, and at some particular time."[3]

With this sound advice in mind, we will focus on

worship as an *act*. Consider three spheres of worship.

CORPORATE WORSHIP

Probably the church's most important act of worship takes place when the people of God come together as one to magnify the Lord in unison.

Granted, there are some who belittle the value of public worship. They retreat to their own individualistic Christianity—a one-man ministry with a one-man membership. Some retreat to their television set and imagine they are in church by joining a TV pastor for thirty minutes. But thirty minutes of electrical waves cannot equal Christian worship. Hebrews 10:25 reminds us that Christians should not forsake "the assembling of [themselves] together, as is the manner of some." Neglect of worship is a bad habit and hurts the individual as well as the unity of the church.

How can corporate worship be lost? This can happen in several ways.

First, corporate worship can be lost *when it becomes dull and joyless.*

More often than not, the reason for dull worship is that the Lord Jesus Christ has been left out. The cure for dull worship is to worship God in all His fullness as Father, Son, and Holy Spirit.

Second, corporate worship can be lost *when it becomes lopsided and heavy* with emotionalism or intellectualism.

Instead of being a full-orbed adventure engaging the intellect, emotions, and will, worship is reduced to sheer emotionalism, or sheer intellectualism. For some, worship becomes sheer volunteerism. God gave us a mind *to know Him*, a heart *to love Him*, and a will *to obey Him*. In biblical worship, all three must be involved. We need all three in balance.

Third, corporate worship can be lost when *it becomes thoughtless or hurried.*

We can't expect flowers to bloom on Sunday morning if the ground hasn't been prepared and watered during the week. It's important to *prepare ourselves for church worship* at least the night before. It is also important to retire early on Saturday so that we are rested for the Lord's Day. You might try taking your seat in church ten minutes before the service begins in order to read the text and seek the Lord in prayer. We need corporate worship in all its magnificence, for without it, we sabotage the church and our individual growth.

ELEMENTS OF CORPORATE WORSHIP

What do we do when we come together? We praise the Lord. Colossians 3:16 suggests some of the elements of worship: "teaching and admonishing one another in psalms and hymns and spiritual songs, singing with grace in your hearts to the Lord."

What else do we do? We devote ourselves to the apostle's teaching, to fellowship, to the breaking of bread, and to prayer, as the early Christians did in Acts 2:42. We expect God to work among us. That is what corporate worship is all about.

Not long ago, a friend complained to me that he was disappointed with the worship of his church. He considered not going to church at all, and he sought my advice.

"What do you do for your own personal worship?" I asked.

"Nothing," was his reply.

Then I asked him, "What are you doing in your family worship?"

Again, he answered, "Nothing."

Finally, I gave him some advice. I said, "You can't expect the church to do for you what you are unwilling to do for yourself. Take care of these other areas, and you'll be more prepared to make a contribution to the worship of your church."

INDIVIDUAL WORSHIP

Corporate worship is not the only act of worship. Individual worship is indispensable. Sometimes we call this by other names. We refer to it as our "quiet time," or "morning watch," or "devotions." Whatever the name, the principle is the same. We worship God at set times each day to give Him our plans and re-acknowledge His lordship.

Here is a discipline we can't live without. No Christian in all of church history has been able to continue the Christian life and neglect individual worship! The prophet Daniel had daily set times of prayer. So did Jesus. In Mark 1:35 we learn that early in the morning Jesus went to a solitary place to pray. If it was important enough for Jesus, then it is certainly necessary for you and me! Every member of Christ's church needs to take time for individual worship. The psalmist reminds us: "Be still, and know that I am God" (Psalm 46:10).

In Romans 12, the apostle Paul urges us to "present [our] bodies a living sacrifice, holy, acceptable to God, which is [our] reasonable service" (v. 1). As someone has said, the trouble with a living sacrifice is that it keeps crawling off the altar. That's just the point. We need to present and re-present ourselves daily to the Lord.

What does the apostle mean by the word *present*? Paul goes on to explain it in verses 2–21. It involves renewing our minds (v. 2), humbling ourselves (v. 3), committing our gifts to Him (vv. 4–8), making love our aim (v. 9), and hating evil and clinging to what is good (v. 9). Presenting ourselves means daily resetting our priorities in the light of Jesus Christ and the Bible.

What should be the pattern of our individual worship? There's no set pattern. In fact, it's good to vary patterns. But there are three key elements that each of us should keep in mind.

ELEMENTS OF INDIVIDUAL WORSHIP

First, *praise*. Praise fills our mind with right thoughts. It clears our affections. As the psalmist said, "I will sing praise to Your name forever, that I may daily perform my vows" (Psalm 61:8).

Second, *prayer*. Most of the time I pray extemporaneously. But I do have an outline in my head that helps me. I often take the word ACTS as a reminder.

A is for *adoration*—high praise for God's Person. *C* is for *confession*—an honest naming of my sins and a new resolve to follow Christ. *T* is for *thanksgiving*—verbal appreciation for all God's works, particularly as they touch my life. And *S* is for *supplication*—petitions for people, events, and things.

Another reminder I use is the word SPACE: *S*—is there *a sin* to confess? *P*—is there *a promise* to claim? *A*—is there *an attitude* to change? *C*—is there *a command* to obey? *E*—is there *an example* to follow?

There are some times, though, when I need help praying. So I use the Lord's Prayer and the many other prayers of the Bible. The psalms are indispensable for me. I don't think I could make it without the psalms.

Third, *Scripture*. We need to read the Bible. Come to it with prayerful, hungry hearts. Ask the Lord to teach you. Next, ask yourself what God is saying to you through the Bible.

Praise, prayer, and Scripture are essential elements of our individual worship.

FAMILY WORSHIP

In addition to corporate worship and individual worship, we need family worship. Spend time regularly as a couple or as a family to cultivate and enjoy God's presence. This is one of the most overlooked responsibilities that God requires of families. Family worship involves Bible reading, study, prayer, and praise. It accelerates spiritual growth.

In the Old Testament, the promises of God extended to Abraham and his seed. The New Testament includes children as part of the visible church. Oddly enough, there is no mention of youth groups or youth pastors in the Bible. Perhaps that is because Scripture assumes that parents are the primary youth pastors of the church. Parents are responsible to raise their children in the Lord.

The foundation of this responsibility is seen in the Old Testament. Deuteronomy 6:1–9 instructs parents to teach their children the commands of God: "You shall teach them diligently to your children, and shall talk of them when you sit in your house, when you walk by the way, when you lie down, and when you rise up" (v. 7).

This passage suggests the *when* and *how* of family worship. The *when* is clear: "When you sit in your house . . . walk by the way . . . lie down, and when you rise up." Moses then told the people the *how* of their worship: "You shall bind them as a sign on your hand.

. . . You shall write them on the doorposts" (vv. 8–9). Both formally and informally, we can impress upon our families the significance of worship.

In the first eight chapters of Proverbs we learn how parents taught children to fear God. "My son, hear the instruction of your father, and do not forsake the law of your mother" (Proverbs 1:8).

Let's remember that the smallest cell group in the church is the family. The home is a little church. Its heads are ministers. Parents are to bring their children up in the discipline and instruction of the Lord (see Ephesians 6:4).

HOW TO BEGIN FAMILY WORSHIP

How should parents initiate family worship? Let me suggest several ways.

First, realize that family worship is not a cure-all. Effective family worship takes place in an environment where parents live out their faith. When parents' deeds don't match their words, negative growth actually occurs. Remember, you can't pass on what you don't possess.

Second, conduct worship with the ages and needs of your children in mind. Vary methods for preschoolers, grade-schoolers, and high schoolers.

Third, be practical and brief.

Fourth, let your times together include praise, prayer, and Scripture. Make it an enjoyable time and try to apply what you learn.

"Worship begins in holy expectancy and ends in holy obedience," Richard Foster wrote.[4] Society is constantly trying to squeeze you and your family into its mold. When the world's input exceeds the input of godliness, then the world wins the battle for the minds and souls of our family.

Worshiping God in spirit and in truth is not optional. It is a necessity. Worship is the one thing a church can do that no other group can do.

Right worship as part of the church, as individuals and as a family is an indispensable part of continuing the Christian life.

QUESTIONS

1. Suggest some possible definitions of worship.
2. What can we do to enhance corporate worship?
3. Discuss some helpful features of individual worship.
4. Read Deuteronomy 6:1–9 and list the principles involved in family worship.

NOTES

1. Warren Wiersbe, *Real Worship* (Nashville: Thomas Nelson, 1986), 21.

2. A. W. Tozer, *Worship: The Missing Jewel of the Evangelical Church* (Camp Hill, Pa.: Christian Publications, 1979).

3. Theodore Roosevelt, in *Day-by-Day with Billy Graham*, Joan Winmill Brown, comp. and ed., February 5 (Minneapolis: World Wide Publications, 1976).

4. Richard Foster, *Celebration of Discipline* (San Francisco: HarperCollins, 1988), 173.

"*Continue* earnestly in prayer,
being vigilant in it with thanksgiving."

COLOSSIANS 4:2 (ITALICS ADDED)

"The great fault of the children of God is, they do not
continue in prayer; . . . they do not persevere. If they
desire anything for God's glory, they should pray until
they get it. Oh, how good, and kind, and gracious, and
condescending is the one with whom we have to do!
He has given me, unworthy as I am, immeasurably
above all I had asked or thought!"

GEORGE MUELLER (EMPHASIS ADDED)

"So when they had appointed elders in every church,
and *prayed with fasting*, they commended them to
the Lord in whom they had believed."

ACTS 14:23 (ITALICS ADDED)

"Fasting should . . . include abstinence
from anything which is legitimate in and of itself,
for the sake of some special spiritual purpose."

MARTIN LLOYD-JONES,
STUDIES IN THE SERMON ON THE MOUNT

4

PRAYER AND FASTING

EVAN ROBERTS, a coal miner and Bible school student, felt burdened for the people of his home church in Wales, Great Britain, in the year 1904. Under the teaching of Seth Joshua, Roberts prayed, "O God, bend me." And God did begin to change him.

While in prayer, twenty-six-year-old Roberts felt led of God to leave school to speak to the people of his home church. His pastor, however, was reluctant to let him speak to the usual Sunday congregation because of the young man's youth and inexperience. He suggested instead that Roberts could speak to those attending the Monday night prayer service. Later, he reneged on that offer and waited until the prayer meeting was over. Then he announced: "Our young brother, Evan Roberts, feels he has a message for the congregation, if any would care to wait and hear him." Seventeen people waited.

Roberts told those who remained afterward at the Moriah Church in Loughor, Wales: "I have a message for you from God. You must confess any known sin to God, and put any wrong done to man right. Second, you must put away any doubtful habit of your life. Third, you must obey the Spirit's prompting. Finally, you must confess your faith in Christ publicly." By 10:00 p. m., all had responded.

The pastor was so pleased that he invited Roberts to speak the following night at a missions service. Young Evan Roberts would pray and preach all week long. A newspaper in the area ran the headline: "Great Crowds of People Are Drawn to Loughor." The writer reported that the road on which the church was situated was packed with people trying to get to the church. Others were closing shops and stores early in order to get a place in the auditorium.[1]

The congregation asked him to stay for another week. Later a reporter arrived from Cardiff and described what he saw: "It was a strange thing," he said. "The service continued throughout the evening and ended at 2:30 in the morning, and even then the people didn't seem willing to go home. The people were still standing outside the church talking about what had happened." The journalist, in typical British understatement, wrote, "I felt this was no ordinary gathering."[2]

The revival swept like a flood over all of Wales, so that soon the churches were full. A local minister reported that the community was converted into a praying multitude. They estimated that over 100,000 people were converted in a five-month period.[3]

The social impact of the awakening was astounding. Judges were presented with white gloves because they had no cases to try: no rapes, no robberies, no murders, no burglaries, no embezzlements—nothing. The Swansea County Police Court announced that there had not been a single charge for drunkenness over the 1905 New Year holiday weekend. In the Welsh metropolis of Cardiff, the police reported a 60 percent decrease in drunkenness and 40 percent fewer people in jail at the new year.[4]

The spiritual awakening began with a young Bible student praying, "O God, bend me."

The Bible reminds us that the first Christians "continued steadfastly . . . in prayers" (Acts 2:42). So must we!

Prayer is an indispensable ingredient for continuing the Christian life.

WHAT IS PRAYER?

A simple definition of prayer is given to us by the prophet Jeremiah: "Call to Me, and I will answer you, and show you great and mighty things, which you do not know" (Jeremiah 33:3). Prayer is *a call*.

According to Romans 8:15, prayer is also *a cry*. Prayer invites God into our experience, much like Jairus inviting Jesus to meet the needs of his dying daughter. He "pleaded earnestly with him" (Mark 5:23 NIV).

John Bunyan has given us a comprehensive definition of prayer:

> Prayer is a sincere, sensible, affectionate pouring out of the heart and soul to God through Jesus Christ in the strength and assistance of the Holy Spirit for such things as God has promised, according to His Word, for the good of the church with submission and faith to the will of God.[5]

Prayer, according to Scripture, should be *sincere*—open, honest, and without hypocrisy (Jeremiah 29:13). Prayer is also *sensible*. It is not a mindless chatter. The word *affectionate* in Bunyan's definition is illustrated by Psalm 42:1–2: "As the deer pants for the water brooks, so pants my soul for You, O God. My soul thirsts for God, for the living God." Can you feel David's heart of affection?

Prayer should be *through Jesus Christ*. It is in the name of Christ we are converted (Acts 4:12). Through His name we receive cleansing (1 John 1:7). Through His name we experience victory (1 Corinthians 15:57). Scripture reminds us, "Whatever you ask *in My name*, that I will do, that the Father may be glorified in the Son" (John 14:13; italics added).

Prayer, according to John Bunyan, is to be offered *in the strength and assistance of the Holy Spirit*. This is crucial, because often we humans don't know *how* to pray. For example, when we are sick, do we pray for health, for healing, or for homegoing?

Romans 8:26 affirms that "we do not know what we should pray for." In those difficult moments, verse 26 assures us, "The Spirit Himself makes intercession for us with groanings which cannot be uttered." Even more, the Holy Spirit, "makes intercession for the saints according to the will of God" (v. 27).

If the Holy Spirit, in our moments of doubt and uncertainty, prays "according to the will of God," so should we.

WHY PRAY?

We should pray because prayer is God's cure for giving up. Isaiah 40:30–31 reminds us: "Even the youths shall faint and be weary, . . . but those who wait on the Lord shall renew their strength." We should not lose heart. We should not give up.

Martin Luther said, "As it is the business of tailors to make clothes, and cobblers to mend shoes, it is the business of Christians to pray."[6]

We should pray because it is God's way to accomplish God's work. God's work is a supernatural work and can only be accomplished by supernatural means (2 Corinthians 3–4). Prayer alone pulls down the strongholds of Satan.

Samuel Chadwick said, "The one concern of Satan is to keep Christians from praying. He fears nothing from prayerless studies, prayerless work, and prayerless religion. He laughs at our toil, mocks at our wisdom, but trembles when we pray."[7]

We should pray because of the example of Jesus. His whole life was one of continual prayer, and even now, in heaven, "He always lives to make intercession for [us]" (Hebrews 7:25).

We should pray because of the example of the New

Testament church. The history of the church as recorded in the Bible illustrates that the church's success was in direct proportion to their faithfulness in prayer.

PRAYER IN ACTS 12

Acts 12 offers an exciting lesson in prayer. Herod Agrippa I, grandson of Herod the Great, had unleashed his might against the followers of Jesus. To placate the ruling majority, "he killed James the brother of John with the sword" (v. 2). James was part of the famous trio: Peter, James, and John. Together, they were with Jesus on the Mount of Transfiguration as well as in the garden of Gethsemane.

Now James has been martyred and Peter is in jail. Not only was Peter in prison, but "four squads of soldiers" guarded him (v. 4). Four groups of four soldiers watched his every move.

But moments of catastrophe often mark the beginning of a brand new day. As a result of Herod's attack, the church gave itself to "constant prayer" (v. 5).

Answers to Prayer (vv. 6–16). The situation appeared hopeless. "When Herod was about to bring him out, that night Peter was sleeping, bound with two chains between two soldiers; and the guards before the door were keeping the prison" (v. 6). So here is Peter—jailed, chained, and surrounded by guards (v. 6). Yet he is able to sleep. This reminds us of the peace God gives amid our trials (Philippians 4:6–7). Suddenly "an angel of the Lord stood by him, and a light shone in the prison; and he struck Peter on the side and raised him up, saying, 'Arise quickly!' And his chains fell off his hands" (Acts 12:7).

Peter was startled by a brilliant light, a whack to his side, a yank to his feet, and the words "Arise quickly!" Immediately, his chains fell off. What a reminder of God's amazing power!

God performs what we can't do, but not what we can do. The angel instructed Peter, "Gird yourself and tie on your sandals. . . . Put on your garment and follow me" (v. 8). In street English, "Fasten your belt, slip on your shoes, grab your coat, and let's split."

But prayer is not a substitute for work. God cares for problems beyond us, while He expects us to do what we're able to do. Again, in verse 10, God's power is demonstrated: "When they were past the first and the second guard posts, they came to the iron gate that leads to the city, which opened to them of its own accord; and they went out and went down one street, and immediately the angel departed from him." Peter, though dazed by the miracle, realized that God had delivered him from his enemies.

As he thought about all that happened, he came to the house of Mary, the mother of John; and many were in there praying (v. 12).

As Peter urgently knocked and announced his presence, a young girl named Rhoda recognized his voice, even though she didn't open the door. Overcome with excitement and filled with joy, she rushed into the room and broke up the prayer meeting, shouting, "Peter's here! Peter's here!" (see v. 14). To which the believers responded, "You're out of your mind" (see v. 15). As they continued to rationalize, Peter kept on knocking. What an indictment against the praying church!

God's Power Displayed (vv. 18–24). First, Peter was miraculously delivered from prison. Second, believers "were astonished" (v. 16) and "the word of God grew and multiplied" (v. 24). Third, "There was no small stir" in the jail (v. 18). The guards were "examined" and executed as Herod ran off to Caesarea (v. 19). Fourth, Herod was judged. He gave a speech in Caesarea, and God struck him dead (vv. 20–23). Herod had killed James with the sword and intended to do the same with Peter, but God stopped him. Recall

God's promise, "'Vengeance is Mine, I will repay,' says the Lord" (Romans 12:19).

What is the greatest need of the church today? Christlike intercessors. Church history affirms that God's work prospers when God's people pray.

What is the greatest need of each individual Christian? The answer is the same: Christlike intercessors.

John Newton was right: "By one hour's intimate access to the throne of grace you may acquire more true spiritual knowledge and comfort than by a day's or a week's converse with the best of men."[8]

The original Christians "continued steadfastly . . . in prayers" (Acts 2:42). May we, too, continue in this discipline, so that our lives will be a holy sacrifice of praise and worship to God.

ALL ABOUT FASTING

Most of us enjoy eating. In fact, we often find ourselves living from meal to meal, looking forward eagerly to the surprises that we find on our table. Important as good eating is, there are times when *not eating* is better, especially for the serious Christian. Strange as it seems, not eating has proven to be a source of enormous strength to many Christians. Fasting can deepen our spiritual lives.

Through fasting, we draw close enough to God to see Him work in dramatic ways. God often changes history. Though this continually happens, only now and then are we close enough to see it happen. Often it involves fasting.

In the early 1950s, Josef Stalin, dictator of the Soviet Union, was preparing a systematic purge of Jews. The pastor of one London church felt greatly burdened upon hearing the news. He shared his concern for God's ancient people with a few prayer groups. Eventually, they decided to set aside a day for prayer and fasting on behalf of the Soviet Jews. Members of the pastor's congregation, as well as other prayer groups, pledged themselves to abstain from food for the day, to pray for a divine solution.

Two weeks later, Stalin suddenly died at the age of seventy-three. Sixteen of the country's most respected doctors had fought to save his life, but without success.

Bible teacher Derek Prince described the happening in *Shaping History through Prayer and Fasting*. He wrote:

Let it be clearly stated that no member of any of our groups prayed for the death of Stalin. We simply trusted God's wisdom for the answer that was needed. Nevertheless, I am convinced that God's answer came in the form of Stalin's death.[9]

The purge against the Soviet Jews was never carried out. Instead, the whole direction of national policy changed. The Soviet Union went through a period of "de-Stalinization," as Stalin himself was publicly denounced by his successors. Ultimately, as we today have witnessed, the whole Soviet communist system collapsed.

The incident especially interested me because the groups involved not only prayed, but they also fasted. All of us pray, but are there times in life when we should fast? I believe there are—if we do it for the right reasons and in a scriptural way.

WHAT IS FASTING?

Fasting is a believer's voluntary abstinence from food for spiritual reasons.

Moses fasted forty days and nights when he received the Ten Commandments (Exodus 34:28). David fasted when he prayed for the life of his infant son (2 Samuel 12:16–17). Many of the prophets fasted (Daniel 9:3). Jesus fasted forty days and forty nights before being tempted in the wilderness (Matthew 4:1–2). Paul fasted during the storm on his way to Rome (Acts 27:21). As a result, the lives of those on board the ship were spared.

Through the centuries, men and women of God have often fasted. In Europe, leaders of great Christian movements such as Martin Luther, John Calvin, John Knox, John Wesley all fasted at key times. In America, educator and preacher Jonathan Edwards fasted, as did missionary David Brainerd and evangelist Charles Finney.

WHY FAST?

The question is a critical one: Why fast? Luther, Calvin and the rest did *not* fast to make God give them something, but as a way of giving themselves more fully to God. Fasting is not a way to pressure God into giving us what we want. It's not a way of earning points or merit.

Fasting primarily changes *us.* It sharpens our perspective. It turns our eyes toward God, sharpens our spiritual vision, and gives priority to our growing walk with God.

Beyond changing individuals, fasting brings change to peoples. In Old Testament times, Jews under the law were commanded to fast once each year on the Day of Atonement. Later, during the Babylonian captivity, Jewish leaders apparently established additional fasts to commemorate special events.

During times of national crisis, public fasts were proclaimed to call the nation to repentance and to pray for God's intervention. Judah's King Jehoshaphat called for such a fast when the country was attacked by Moab and Ammon (2 Chronicles 20:3). The context describes the revival that followed and the miraculous destruction of the invading army.

Ezra proclaimed a fast to seek God's blessing before he returned to rebuild Jerusalem (Ezra 8:21–23). Esther and Mordecai, faced with the annihilation of exiled Jews in Persia, called the threatened people to three days of prayer and fasting (Esther 4:16).

By the time of Jesus, the Pharisees had added ritual fasts to their religious practice. Jesus mentioned the practice of fasting in the parable of the Pharisee and the tax collector, quoting the Pharisee as saying, "I fast twice a week" (Luke 18:12).

Through the centuries, God's people have known two kinds of fasts. One is acceptable; the other, unacceptable. The Bible distinguishes between them in Isaiah 58:1–7. Speaking through Isaiah, God contrasts the fast the people have chosen with "the fast that I have chosen" (v. 6). Man's kind of fast is self-imposed religious ritual —without repentance or concern to do God's will. The fast that God has chosen begins with full obedience and a contrite heart.

Significantly, fasting has played a part in the history of America. As early as 1636, the Plymouth Colony passed a law allowing the governor and his assistants to set "solemn days of humiliation and fasting."[10]

Two years before the American Revolution, a British embargo on the port of Boston brought a call for a day of prayer and fasting in Virginia. George Washington himself wrote in his diary for June 1, 1774, "I went to church and fasted all day."[11]

Midway through the Civil War, the United States Senate passed a resolution asking that President Abraham Lincoln "designate and set apart a day for national prayer and humiliation." In his "Proclamation for a Day of National Humiliation, Fasting and Prayer," President Lincoln included words of confession and repentance as the Civil War raged around them:

We have forgotten God. We have forgotten the gracious hand which preserved us in peace, and multiplied and enriched and strengthened us;

and we have vainly imagined, in the deceitfulness of our hearts, that all these things were produced by some superior wisdom and virtue of our won. We have become too self-sufficient . . . too proud to pray to God that made us![12]

Lincoln proclaimed April 30, 1863 "a day of national humiliation, fasting and prayer." His hope was "that the united cry of the nation will be heard on high, and answered with blessings, no less than the pardon of our national sins, and restoration of our now divided and suffering country, to its former happy condition of unity and peace."[13]

A PATTERN FOR TODAY

Is fasting for today? Jesus did not command His followers to fast. However, it seems clear that *He expected fasting.* Early in His ministry, in reply to John's disciples, Jesus said His followers would not fast while He was with them. "But the days will come," He said, "when the bridegroom will be taken away from them, and then they will fast in those days" (Mark 2:20).

Jesus also spoke of fasting in His Sermon on the Mount. He spoke of a proper attitude in giving alms, in praying, and in fasting (Matthew 6).

Jesus' language is clear. He does not say "*If* you fast," but "*When* you fast " (vv. 16–18; emphasis added).

Fasting in the early church provides an example for today. We should fast at special times for special reasons. That's how the New Testament church prepared for their first missionaries. Acts 13:2 states that while the leaders of the church in Antioch "ministered to the Lord and fasted," the Holy Spirit told them to send Paul and Barnabas. The whole church prayed and fasted before sending out those two missionaries (v. 3). Later, Paul and Barnabas prayed and fasted before establishing leaders in the missionary churches (Acts 14:23).

Paul mentions fasting as part of the pattern of his apostolic life. "We commend ourselves as ministers of God . . . in stripes, in imprisonments, in tumults, in labors, in sleeplessness, in fastings." (2 Corinthians 6:4–5). Later, when he sums up his labors, he includes the phrase "in fastings often" (2 Corinthians 11:27). Nowhere in the New Testament, however, do we find a command to fast.

WHAT SHOULD BE
THE FOCUS OF OUR FAST?

Some fast in times of personal or family crisis. Others fast to seek God's leading, to pray for those in special need, or to seek God's moving in their church or His blessing on the nation. Some fast once or twice each year as they feel led. During such times they give themselves to prayer, Bible reading, and waiting on God.

Writing in a Christian magazine several years ago, a pastor told what fasting meant to his congregation. Among the outcomes: unusual spiritual growth, a more intimate walk with God, a new love for one another, and a deeper hunger for God and His Word. "One reason," he wrote, "might be that members fast and pray each week for the ministry of the church."

Some members of the church were also enthusiastic about what fasting meant to them personally. For example, a discouraged college senior in the congregation had no idea what to do with his life. After three days of fasting and meditating on the Word of God, he sensed God's leading him into the ministry.

At first, a young business executive was unable to fast for even one full day. He later moved to fasting once a week, as he said, "Simply allowing God to speak." "Not only has something happened to my personal walk with God," this man told his pastor, "but I have never felt better physically."

CAN FASTING HELP?

Can fasting help? Yes. Fasting breaks the pattern of everyday life in which fleshly desires hold the upper hand. It also can help deepen our relationship with Jesus Christ. Fasting helps overcome the barrier of our fleshly nature. Some people find that fasting quickens both the mind and heart. They become more closely attuned to God. They pray with greater power. A time of fasting helps us focus on spiritual values. They take more time for prayer and Bible study. Their spiritual life, which often is neglected, enjoys priority.

You can fast for various reasons. You can fast for victory over some temptation. Or you can use fasting for confession and personal cleansing and renewal. You can fast for a better spiritual life.

You can fast to intercede for others who are spiritually enslaved. There are many with urgent needs that seem untouched by normal times of prayer. Fasting invites intercession with more than ordinary power.

SOME WORDS OF CAUTION

As you consider whether to fast and, if so, how to fast, here are some words of caution. Be sure to fast and pray only for the things you know are in the will of God. If something is outside His will, fasting will never change it.

Don't fast without a reason. Set your heart to do the will of God, to give yourself more fully to Jesus Christ, to continue advancing in the Christian life.

If you fast, it should be voluntary and private. Be careful not to seem to boast in your piety. Jesus said, "When you fast, do not be like the hypocrites," who fast openly to receive the reward of men. Rather, "anoint your head and wash you face; so that you do not appear to men to be fasting, but to your Father who is in the secret place; and your Father who sees in secret will reward you openly" (Matthew 6:16–18).

Motives are essential. We shouldn't fast with the motive of becoming super-spiritual. Fasting is not a means of gaining merit but a means of opening ourselves to God. In addition, we shouldn't fast with the thought that the body is evil—our bodies are the temple of the Holy Spirit.

If you have a physical problem, or if you are

expecting a child, do not begin a fast without consulting with your doctor. In normal circumstances, however, fasting benefits the body. Medical experts say that short fasts not only rest the digestive system but bring about a natural way of eliminating substances harmful to the body. In fact, many people fast for physical reasons only.

Your first fast might be short—a meal or two, or perhaps a day. It is wise to drink water or some other liquid freely. It is unwise to abstain from water for any length of time. If possible, choose a day when work demands are light. Ideally, spend much time in prayer and Bible reading. You may temporarily feel weak or faint, but this reaction will go away. Soon, your body will adjust and you will probably have little or no craving for food.

Finally, remember not to end your fast abruptly. Eat lightly at first. Then follow later with more solid food.

IS FASTING FOR YOU?

It probably is. Only you can decide, of course. But for those who have a sense of deep spiritual need, who seriously want to "lay hold of that for which Christ Jesus has also laid hold" of them (Philippians 3:12), fasting can be effective. Fasting is for those who can do it humbly, without pride.

Undertaken rightly, fasting can be a significant step to an overflowing life as you continue with Christ.

QUESTIONS

1. What is prayer? Suggest several biblical definitions.
2. Suggest several elements involved in biblical prayer. (Refer to John Bunyan's definition.)
3. List several reasons why we should pray as well as a scriptural illustration of the effectiveness of prayer.
4. What is fasting, and is it for Christians today?

NOTES

1. Edwin Orr, *The Flaming Tongue* (Chicago: Moody, 1975), 8.

2. Ibid., 9.

3. J. V. Morgan, *The Welsh Religious Revival* (London: n.p., 1909), 248 ff, as cited in Orr, *The Flaming Tongue*, 15.

4. Ibid., 18.

5. John Bunyan, in *More Gathered Gold*, ed. John Blanchard (United Kingdom: Evangelical Press, 1984), 228.

6. Martin Luther, as quoted in *More Gathered Gold,* 227.

7. Samuel Chadwick in *Draper's Book of Quotations for the Christian World*, comp. Edythe Draper (Wheaton: Tyndale, 1992), 493–94.

8. John Newton, in *Voice of the Heart: Cardiphonia* (Chicago: Moody, 1952), 35.

9. Derek Prince, *Shaping History through Prayer and Fasting* (Old Tappan, N. J.: Revell, 1973), 67.

10. Ibid., 137.

11. Ibid., 138–39.

12. Abraham Lincoln, "A Proclamation for A Day of National Humiliation Fasting and Prayer," March 13, 1863, cited in Prince, *Shaping History*, 2nd ed. (New Kensington, Pa.: Whitaker House, 2002), 11–13.

13. Ibid.

"But you must *continue* in the things which
you have learned and been assured of,
knowing from whom you have learned them."

2 TIMOTHY 3:14 (ITALICS ADDED)

"If I were the devil, one of my first aims would be to
stop folk from digging into the Bible . . . I should do all
I could to surround it with the spiritual
equivalent of pits, thorn hedges, and man traps,
to frighten people off."

J. I. PACKER
FOREWORD, *KNOWING SCRIPTURE*

"Those who seldom read the Bible are very much
like those who have no Bible at all."

UNKNOWN

5

GOING DEEPER INTO THE WORD OF GOD

TO THE WRITERS of the New Testament, the Word of God was indispensable, far more important than daily food. Peter reminds us that we are born again "through the word of God which lives and abides forever" (1 Peter 1:23). We are not only *made alive* by the Word of God, we are *kept alive* by the Word of God. The Bible is God's authoritative revelation to you and me. It is our blueprint and guidebook for continuing the Christian life. When the Bible speaks, God speaks.

But the phrase "Word of God" is not as simple as it appears at first glance. The phrase is used in at least three ways in the New Testament.

"Word of God" sometimes refers to *Jesus*. He is the living Word who became flesh at Bethlehem. Second, "Word of God" can refer to *the preaching of the gospel.* Third, "Word of God" also refers to *the written revelation of Holy Scripture.* Each aspect is important as we continue the Christian life.

THE WORD OF GOD IN CHRIST

The author of the book of Hebrews reminds us that God has spoken to us through Jesus, *the living Word of God*: "God, who at various times and in various ways spoke in time past to the fathers by the prophets, has in these last days spoken to us *by His Son*" (Hebrews 1:1–2; italics added).

In other words, Jesus is God's clearest Word to you and me. His life, death, and resurrection are the heart of what God wants to tell us. Jesus is God's personal Word to us. If we want to see God's clearest expression to a lost world, then we must look at Jesus. All apostolic preaching pointed to Jesus. It's the same with Scripture. The Old and New Testaments both point to Jesus.

In John 5:39–40, Jesus warned those who pursued Scripture apart from Himself as an end in itself. "You search the Scriptures," He said, "for in them you think you have eternal life; and these are they which testify of Me. But you are not willing to come to Me that you may have life."

Jesus was referring to the ancient Jewish authorities, who studied the Law and the Prophets and yet rejected Him as Messiah. We, too, can fall into the same trap. Bible study can become an end in itself. We can fail to let the written Word lead us to Jesus, the living Word. Unlike the Hebrew authorities, the early Christians searched the Scriptures specifically—specifically—to see Jesus in them.

The apostle John writes in the prologue of his gospel: "In the beginning was the Word" (John 1:1). John points to the eternal relationship that existed between God the Father and God the Son.

John continues: "And the Word was *with God*" (all italics added). The point here is that the Word is a person distinct from God the Father. Then John adds the phrase, "and the Word *was God*," which announces the true deity of Jesus, who shares the Father's nature.

In verse 14, John brings the prologue to a stunning climax by stating, "The Word became flesh and dwelt among us, and we beheld His glory."

God's self-disclosure was not vague nor hidden, but vivid and personal. Just imagine what would have happened to Adam's love life had God given him a photograph of Eve, and not the real person. Or imagine Adam's reaction if God had given him only a written description of Eve and not Eve herself. Adam would have been frustrated. But God did nothing of the kind. Rather, He gave Adam a beautiful, striking woman and told them to become one flesh.

And God's revelation of Himself is that real. He didn't send a picture, nor did He limit His revelation to a written message. He actually took on human flesh, became a man, and demonstrated His love before our very eyes. He wanted us to see and better understand the glory, the grace, and the truth of God.

To continue *the Christian life it's essential to focus on Jesus.* Study His person and works. Let no spiritual gift or experience or social agenda take the place of Jesus. Let Jesus Himself be your passion, for the mystery of our faith lies here.

Paul told the Colossians that Jesus "is the image of the invisible God" (Colossians 1:15). "He is before all things, and in Him all things consist" (v. 17). "He is the head of the body, the church, . . . [and is] the firstborn from the dead." (v. 18). In Him "are hidden all the treasures of wisdom and knowledge" (2:3). He is to have first place, not second, "that in all things He may have the preeminence" (1:18).

So, each of us needs to ask ourself, "Do I have a

growing relationship with Jesus, the living Word of God?"

THE WORD OF GOD IN PREACHING

The phrase "Word of God" can also refer to the gospel preached by the apostles. It's the saving message of Jesus.

The disciples spoke the Word of God "with boldness" (Acts 4:31). In Acts 6:7, we learn of the growth of the early church and how the Word of God kept on spreading. In Acts 13:5, we're told that Paul and Barnabas "preached the word of God in the synagogues of the Jews." These passages do not refer directly to Jesus the incarnate Word, but rather to the *preached Word of God.*

In Romans 10:13–14, Paul proclaimed: "'Whoever calls on the name of the Lord shall be saved.' How then shall they call on Him in whom they have not believed? And how shall they believe in Him of whom they have not heard? And how shall they hear without a preacher?"

Paul immediately answers his own question: "So then faith comes by hearing, and hearing *by the word of God*" (Romans 10:17, italics added). This Word of God was the content of apostolic teaching and preaching.

Do not think of apostolic preaching as the apostles slowly grinding their way through heavy, tedious, theology. Apostolic preaching didn't put people to sleep. To the contrary, their audiences either picked up stones to hurl at them or they cried out for salvation. Wherever the Word of God was preached, supernatural power was unleashed.

And so today, our preaching should throb with the same power. To continue the Christian life, each of us needs to be exposed regularly to the systematic teaching of the Word of God. The church will grow only through the ministry of the Word of God. The end of preaching is the conversion and edification of souls. This is why each of us needs a regular diet of expository preaching. The preacher takes the Word of God and applies it to the human situation. He preaches plainly in the demonstration of the Holy Spirit and power. He makes known the whole counsel of God and wisely applies it to his listeners. His delivery is marked by a fervent love for God and a passion for souls. He aims at God's glory.

Not only do we need to expose ourselves to the proclamation of the Word of God, we need to *prepare* ourselves to hear the Word of God regularly. Our hearts need to be primed and our sins confessed before we hear God's Word. We need to be ready to receive the message with faith and meekness.

After the preaching, we ought to question each other about what we heard. Our first question as we review the service ought to be, "How did God speak to me today?"—not, "What did you think of the message?"

To successfully continue the Christian life, we must faithfully submit to the proclaimed Word of God.

THE WORD OF GOD IN SCRIPTURE

In addition to the Word of God *in Christ* and the Word of God *in preaching*, we must lay hold of the Word of God *in Scripture*. Scripture informs our living and teaching. It gives us the earliest statements of the gospel and the broadest statement of God's truth.

Scripture also informs us of Jesus. It contains the best records of His life. We can't know Jesus apart from Scripture. Attempts to separate the two will always fail. Luther called Scripture "the cradle of Christ."

What is Scripture? It is the Bible, God's verbal revelation to man. Augustine called it "a letter of God Almighty addressed to His creatures." In the Bible, God speaks through the human words of patriarchs, prophets, and apostles. By His Holy Spirit, He inspired them to say exactly what He wanted to say. He used their personalities and situations in such a way that His message for all time could come to us—and without error. This inspiration extends to the very words of the Bible, so that we may think of its words as God's words. What Scripture says, God says!

What should our attitude be toward Scripture? We should display reverent, joyful obedience. We should copy the attitude of Jesus. He placed the authority of Scripture first—before the traditions and philosophies of men. Jesus knew that the Old Testament, His Bible, was the Word of His Father. Jesus based His life on the Scriptures. It was His guide for moral conduct. It was His authority in controversies. It was His text in preaching. It was His poetry. It was His wisdom. It was the map of His life.

Loyalty to Jesus as our lord and teacher demands that we follow His example. Jesus approached Scripture with a believing, obedient spirit.

It's important to remember that Jesus avoided the two mistaken views of Scripture prevalent in His day. On the one hand, He did not agree with the Sadducees. The Sadducees judged Scripture by their reason, making Scripture subservient to reason. They did not accept all of the Old Testament. They chose the parts that appealed to them. In this way they are like those theological liberals today who place the human mind above the mind of God. Jesus rejected this view. For Him, reason was subservient to Scripture.

On the other hand, Jesus did not agree with the Pharisees, either. The Pharisees put human tradition on the same level as the authority of Scripture. Theirs was a two-source theory of authority. Yet, we know from the New Testament that their traditions smothered the written Word of God.

The Pharisees have their counterparts today. According to some, Scripture and tradition are of equal weight. But we must take our cue from Jesus, who criticized the Pharisees in Mark 7:13 for "making the word of God of no effect through your tradition." This is what inevitably happens when the traditions of men are given equal weight to the words of God. Martin Luther thundered against this error in the sixteenth century. He stood, as we must stand today, on the authority of the Word of God *alone*.

We should read Scripture not only out of loyalty to Jesus, but also because *the Bible is the guidebook of our life* with God. It's a lamp to our feet and a light to our path (Psalm 119:105). It is the sword of the Spirit

(Hebrews 4:12). D. L. Moody once remarked, "I never saw a useful Christian who was not a student of the Bible."[1]

Paul reminded Timothy, "All Scripture is given by inspiration of God, and is profitable for doctrine, for reproof, for correction, for instruction in righteousness, that the man of God may be complete, thoroughly equipped for every good work" (2 Timothy 3:16–17).

Scripture is essential for continuing the Christian life. What we believe about the Bible is one of the most crucial issues a Christian faces. If you accept its authority as supreme, as Jesus did, then it's your duty to submit to it as well. A high view of Scripture is meaningless unless we actually read its pages, believe its promises, and live out its commands. As D. L. Moody said, "A man can no more take in a supply of grace for the future than he can eat enough food for the next six months, or take sufficient air into his lungs at one time to sustain him for a week. We must draw upon God's boundless store of grace day by day as we need it."

OUR RESPONSIBILITY TO
KNOW THE WORD OF GOD

God has spoken one consistent word to us in a threefold way. Think of these three aspects of the Word of God as the target of an archer. The bull's-eye of God's Word is *Jesus*—God's personal Word to you. Each ring in the target draws our attention to Jesus. The next circle of God's Word is the *gospel*—the proclaimed Word. The ring next to that is the wider circle of the *Holy Spirit*—God's written Word. To continue in the Christian life, we need God's Word in all its fullness, beauty, and power. Each of us needs to experience God's Word in this threefold way.

But what should we *do* with God's Word once we receive Jesus and accept the truth of His gospel and submit our lives to the teaching of Scripture? Let me urge three important steps: We must *know the Word of God, do the Word of God,* and *share the Word of God.*

Press on in your knowledge and love of Christ. Understand the gospel in more than a superficial way. Study the doctrines of grace, atonement, sin, and salvation. And then drink deeply from the well of the Scriptures daily so that your thoughts are saturated with the very words of God.

KNOWING GOD'S WORD
THROUGH BIBLE STUDY

Going deeper in the Word of God can be accomplished only by serious study of the Scripture on a regular basis.

Bible study is a must for spiritual growth. Repeatedly, we are encouraged in the Scriptures to grow in "grace and knowledge" (2 Peter 3:18). Peter also instructs all believers to grow "as newborn babes, [desiring] the pure milk of the word, that you may grow thereby" (1 Peter 2:2).

But how do we grow? Paul told the Colossians: "As you therefore have received Christ Jesus the Lord, so walk in Him, rooted and built up in Him and established in the faith" (Colossians 2:6–7). He gave similar instruction to the church at Ephesus: "I commend you to God and to the word of His grace, which is able to build you up" (Acts 20:32). The Bible read and studied builds us up and enables us to go deeper in the things of God.

Bible study equips us for the struggles of life. Have you experienced difficulty regarding sinful thoughts or behavior? It is the Word of God that equips us and preserves us. David asks, "How can a young man cleanse his way? By taking heed according to Your word" (Psalm 119:9). Filling the mind with the Word of God is the divine method to equip us for life's battles.

Bible study prepares Christians for service. The Old Testament tells us how Joshua was prepared by God for a successful ministry: "This Book of the Law shall not depart from your mouth, but you shall meditate in it day and night, that you may observe to do according to all that is written in it. For then you will make your way prosperous, and then you will have good success" (Joshua 1:8).

Joshua's priority was to meditate on God's Word by day and by night. These verses remind me of Psalm 1, which tells of the godly person who delights "in the law of the Lord" and "meditates [on it] day and night" (v. 2).

Needless to say, to continue the Christian life, we must go deeper in the Word of God. It's impossible to become more like Jesus and not be a serious student of Scripture.

In approximately twenty minutes a day, you can read through the Bible in less than a year. Each day I read three chapters in the Old Testament and three chapters in the New Testament, and, in twelve months, I finish the Old Testament once and the New Testament four times.

We also need to study the Word of God if we are to know it. There are many ways to do this. You could study the Bible topically. *Nave's Topical Bible* is helpful. Since I often use the King James Version or the *New King James Version*, I like *Strong's Exhaustive Concordance*, or *Young's Analytical Concordance*, or even *Cruden's Complete Concordance*.

The *New American Standard Exhaustive Concordance* and the *New International Version Exhaustive Concordance* are also invaluable.

Some like to study the Bible biographically, and they find great inspiration and strength in the lives of Bible personalities.

Personally, I enjoy studying a single chapter or a single passage. After reading the context, I'll read the passage three or four times. Then, I like to focus on special words until I feel I truly understand what has been written. I look for the main theme and supporting traits. Finally, I write out a personal application. In other words, what does this passage say to me today?

If I'm planning to teach a particular passage, I'll also consult other commentaries and word studies to profit from the instruction of others. The main difference between Bible reading and Bible study is an in-depth effort to *write out and think through what has been read.* The very exercise of writing focuses our interest and greatly increases our retention.

Last, regardless of your age, I would encourage you to *memorize the Word of God* (see Psalm 119:11). Scripture stored in the mind is available to the Holy Spirit to teach us even when our mind is weary or confused. The memorized Word of God strengthens our faith. It is a source of guidance in God's will and it stimulates spiritual maturity.

Those who seldom read the Bible are very much like those who have no Bible at all.

YIELD TO AND SHARE THE WORD OF GOD

Submit to Jesus, the Lord. Give Him every area of your life. Bow to the truth and the sure knowledge of the gospel so that your mind will not waver about your salvation and your service. Yield to the whole counsel of God in Scripture as the Holy Spirit applies its truths to your life. "Be doers of the word, and not hearers only" (James 1:22).

Let all that you do proclaim Jesus Christ, His gospel, and the truth of God found in the Bible daily.

To continue the Christian life requires *knowing*

the Word, *doing* the Word, and *sharing* the Word. John MacArthur's testimony is true:

> The greatest thing that ever happened in my life, next to my salvation, occurred when I learned to study the Word of God night and day. While I haven't arrived, by any stretch of the imagination, I have learned this—that the longer and more intensely and more devotedly I look into the face of God, the more God changes my life into the image of His Son. Bible Study has become the passion of my heart for my own life.[2]

QUESTIONS

1. List three ways in which the phrase "Word of God" is used in the Bible.
2. Why is it important to understand that Jesus is the living Word of God?
3. How is the Bible God's verbal revelation to mankind?
4. What are individual Christians to do with the Word of God?
5. Suggest four reasons Bible study is indispensable to continuing the Christian life.

NOTES

1. D. L. Moody, in Don Sweeting and George Sweeting, *Lessons from the Life of Moody* (Chicago: Moody, 1989), 129.

2. John MacArthur, *Keys to Spiritual Growth* (Old Tappan, N.J.: Revell, 1978), 19.

"I will *continue* with all of you
for your progress and joy in the faith."

PHILIPPIANS 1:25 (NIV, ITALICS ADDED)

"The Spirit-filled life is no mystery revealed to a select
few, no goal difficult of attainment. To trust and obey
is the substance of the whole matter."

V. RAYMOND EDMAN,
QUOTATIONS FOR THE CHRISTIAN WORLD

"But the Helper, the Holy Spirit, whom the Father will
send in My name, He will teach you all things,
and bring to your remembrance
all things that I said to you."

JOHN 14:26

6

THE ROLE OF THE HOLY SPIRIT IN CHRISTIAN GROWTH

A CHAMELEON IS a lizard-like creature that has the ability to change the color of its skin to match its surroundings. If this creature rests on a green surface, it appears green in color. Against wood bark it looks gray or black, and against soil it assumes the color of the earth.

Someone humorously related how a chameleon crawled onto a piece of Scottish plaid and exploded . . . trying to make good.

Each of us know people who are very much like chameleons. In the locker room, they behave differently than in their homes or in church. At their place of work, they blend in with their fellow workers in hurtful conduct. However, Jesus never called His followers to be chameleons.

God calls us to a superior life and provides all that is necessary for us to increasingly become like Jesus. This is the role of God the Holy Spirit. God not only calls us to be holy, He helps us to be holy.

In John's gospel, Jesus said, "If you love Me, *keep* My commandments" (John 14:15, all italics added). Jesus said virtually the same thing in verse 21 of the chapter, except in a slightly different way: "He who has My commandments and *keeps them*, it is he who loves Me. And he who loves Me will be loved by My Father, and I will love him and *manifest Myself to him.*"

Because the call to live a Spirit-filled life is beyond our human ability, God reminds us that He will love us and "manifest" Himself to us. Jesus then added, in verse 23, "If anyone loves Me, he will keep My word; and My Father will love him, and We will come to him and make Our home with him."

THE HOLY SPIRIT IS OUR HELPER

One of the names for the Holy Spirit is "Helper" (John 14:16; "Comforter," KJV; "Counselor," NIV). Jesus, of course, is our first helper (Philippians 4:13). But the Holy Spirit is also our helper (John 14:26).

Before Jesus went to the cross, He prayed that God the Father would send to His followers "another Helper"

(John 14:16, 26; 15:26; 16:7). The Greek word is *parakletos*, meaning "one who helps, encourages, and strengthens." The Holy Spirit is a person, not an influence, and as such, He is to be obeyed, loved, and worshiped along with God the Father and God the Son.

Continuing the Christian life is impossible apart from the help of the Holy Spirit. The Holy Spirit enlightens us (Ephesians 1:17–18), regenerates us (John 3:5–8), enables us to become holy (Romans 8:13–14), changes us (2 Corinthians 3:18), provides us assurance (Romans 8:16), and blesses us with gifts for service (1 Corinthians 12:4–11). All that God does for us is accomplished through God the Holy Spirit.

We live in a man-centered world that underscores the latent power within each individual. This is the constant theme of most of the self-help books. However, the Bible calls for something infinitely better: Holy Spirit help. Self-help alone is destined to disappoint you. The life of the Spirit is supernatural and not of self.

THE HOLY SPIRIT CONNECTS US TO JESUS IN SALVATION

The Holy Spirit strives with us as the Spirit of conviction, moving us to the place of repentance and faith.

The Holy Spirit came not only to reveal "the deep things of God" to us (1 Corinthians 2:10), but to convict the world of sin, righteousness, and judgment (John 16:8). The role of the Holy Spirit with mankind is that of revealing God's truth in such a way as to bring us to faith in Jesus Christ.

The words of Jesus to Nicodemus are very clear in John 3:3–6:

> Jesus answered and said to him, "Most assuredly, I say to you, unless one is born again, he cannot see the kingdom of God." Nicodemus said to Him, "How can a man be born when he is old? Can he enter a second time into his mother's womb and be born?" Jesus answered, "Most assuredly, I say to you, unless one is born of water and the Spirit, he cannot enter the kingdom of God. That which is born of the flesh is flesh, and that which is born of the Spirit is spirit."

Jesus reminds us in this passage that flesh gives birth to flesh and apart from a supernatural birth, we cannot see or enter the kingdom of God.

THE HOLY SPIRIT CONFORMS US TO THE LIKENESS OF JESUS

Have you ever wondered why the Holy Spirit is called *Holy*? The attribute of holiness belongs to each member of the Trinity, yet we do not call them "Holy Father" or "Holy Son."

The Holy Spirit is called *Holy* because that's His primary role for each believer in Christ. He is the one who sanctifies us. It is His job to make us holy. He connects us to the ongoing work and life of Jesus. He conforms us to the very likeness of Christ (see Romans 8:29).

Philippians 2:12 calls on each follower of Jesus to "work out your own salvation with fear and trembling." The call to a holy life is a serious challenge and requires a sincere commitment. However, Paul continues in this passage to tell us that we can succeed only through God's supernatural work. "It is God who works in you both to will and to do for His good pleasure" (v. 13). In ourselves, the struggle is hopeless. However, the Holy Spirit encourages our new desires and purposes, even though our flesh seeks to hinder us from being all that God requires. It is by watching, praying, and submitting that we can enjoy victory. In the strength of the Holy Spirit we can "put to death the deeds of the body" (Romans 8:13; see also Colossians 3:5).

It is through the work of the Holy Spirit that we become new creatures in Christ. He quickens us so that we are made alive (John 3:3–5; 2 Corinthians 3:6; Titus 3:5). Following conversion, the Holy Spirit indwells each believer. We become the very dwelling places of God (Romans 8:9; 1 Corinthians 3:16; 6:19).

THE HOLY SPIRIT LEADS BELIEVERS THROUGH THE WORD OF GOD

The Holy Spirit guides us in a growing realization and appreciation of God the Father and God the Son. He enables us to know God in a deeper, more intimate way.

It's important to remember that the Holy Spirit never leads anyone to believe or do anything contrary to the Scripture. Rather, He teaches us through the Word of God as we respond in obedience. We do well to remember that the Holy Spirit is the author of the Word of God and gave special gifts and qualifications to the human authors of the Bible (1 Corinthians 12:4, 8–11, 28-29). He inspired, or "breathed out," the Scriptures in their entirety through the use of men (2 Timothy 3:16). He is also the interpreter of the Bible (John16:13–14; Ephesians 1:17). The Holy Spirit is indispensable to continued Christian growth.

In order for any human to survive physically, our bodies need an abundance of liquids. Personally, I begin each day with a glass of water and a glass of orange juice, and often a cup or two of coffee. However, I drink fluids continually all day long. To operate successfully, we need fluids throughout the day. To the woman of Samaria, Jesus said, "Whoever drinks of this water will thirst again, but whoever drinks of the water that I shall give him will never thirst" (John 4:13–14).

Paul the apostle compares the life of the Spirit to drinking. To survive and thrive in the Christian life, we must drink deeply of the Spirit of God.

THE FILLING OF THE SPIRIT

In Ephesians 5:18, Paul offers a life-changing challenge to each follower of Christ: "Do not be drunk with wine, in which is dissipation; but be filled with the Spirit." Being drunk with wine means being given over to the influence of wine. Paul is drawing a parallel here. Being filled with the Spirit of God means to be given over to the Holy Spirit's influence. This simply means that we are led and directed by God the Holy Spirit.

Several things should be observed concerning Ephesians 5:18. First, the words are in the imperative mood. In other words, being filled with the Spirit is not a suggestion or even an appeal, but rather a biblical command. Anything less than the fullness of the Spirit is not in accordance with God's expressed desire.

Second, "be filled" indicates a present, ongoing action. Simply, we are to be filled with the Holy Spirit *now*. It is a continuous action verb that could be translated like this: "being filled with the Spirit." We are to be filled daily, moment by moment. Yesterday's blessings will not do for today or tomorrow. Being filled with the Spirit is not a once-and-for-all event, but rather a way of life.

Filling means control, and control means all the known areas of my life. Such control is the way of Christian growth.

Third, it is a passive verb. That means that being filled with the Spirit is not something we do, but rather *something that God does for us.* Our part is to yield to the Holy Spirit. We must be willing! We must submit! But God does the filling. By faith, we simply receive the results. Being filled means doing what God the Holy Spirit wants us to do, and that filling is maintained by abiding in Christ (John 15:4–10).

The Bible also includes warnings to those who resist or neglect the work of the Holy Spirit. Ephesians 4:30 warns all Christians not to grieve the Holy Spirit. Also, 1 Thessalonians 5:19 cautions believers not to quench His ministry. To *quench* is to cool down, subdue, or extinguish.

A CHOICE TO MAKE

Each of us has a critical choice to make. We can choose to be filled with the Holy Spirit or we can choose to be filled with other pursuits of life.

What is it like to be filled with the Holy Spirit? I believe it is like this: When I awake in the morning, I consciously ask Jesus Christ to order my day. I earnestly pray for wisdom and divine strength for each opportunity and challenge. I ask the Lord to enable me to live in His presence, to guide and accompany me all day long. I pray, "Lord, help me to 'walk . . . according to the Spirit'" (Romans 8:1).

I also fortify myself against evil by reading and remembering the promises of Scripture. I resolve to live today according to the Word of God and according to the guidance of the Holy Spirit (Romans 8:5). I ask the Lord to help me display the fruit of the Holy Spirit (Galatians 5:22), and to manifest the traits of divine wisdom (James 3:17) in all of the details of the day. I also seek to acknowledge my sins and failures quickly and find forgiveness, cleansing, and restoration. I pray, "Lord, may 'the Spirit . . . who raised Jesus from the dead . . . give life to [my] mortal [body]'" (Romans 8:11).

And when my day is done and I lay me down to sleep, I ask the Lord to rule supreme in every area of my life for Jesus' sake.

This is the role of the Holy Spirit in helping the followers of Jesus to continue the Christian life.

QUESTIONS

1. List several names ascribed to the Holy Spirit in the Bible.
2. Why is the Holy Spirit called *Holy*?
3. What is our part in the work of sanctification (Philippians 2:12)?
4. How does the Holy Spirit help believers in Jesus Christ?
5. What does it mean to be filled with the Holy Spirit (Ephesians 5:18)?

"Pursue love."

1 CORINTHIANS 14:1

"Keep yourselves in God's love as you wait
for the mercy of our Lord Jesus Christ
to bring you to eternal life."

JUDE 21(NIV)

"What does love look like? It has the hands to help
others. It has the feet to hasten to the poor and needy.
It has the eyes to see misery and want. It has the ears
to hear the sighs and the sorrows of men.
That is what love looks like."

AUGUSTINE

7

HOW TO BECOME A
LOVE-FILLED PERSON

THERE WAS A TIME in my life when I was afraid of the subject of God's love. I mistakenly thought that an emphasis on God's love was a cop-out for a spineless faith.

My attitude might be partially explained by my Scottish roots. My parents, though godly, caring people, were not given to an external show of emotion. I never saw my father cry. He told us he had forgotten how to cry. And though Mother suffered deeply at times, she would quietly maintain, "We Scots don't wear our feelings on our sleeves."

Not only was I a child of immigrant parents, but I was also endowed with a full head of curly hair. This combination made me an easy target for teasing, so I quickly learned the art of self-defense. Occasionally, when I needed courage, Mother would softly say,

"Laddie, the blood of the covenanters is in your veins." Though I didn't understand all that phrase meant, I was primed to fight the whole neighborhood. It was important to me to be strong, as I saw no future in being dubbed a "softy."

I have since discovered that I was not alone in my misunderstanding of God's love. Few people have a clear idea of what this love really is.

The word *love* has been used to describe so many things that it can be confusing. Sometimes it's used to describe the emotions of romance (and what a marvelous experience that is!). The same word is also used to describe lust, the desire for sexual gratification. At times, it is used to indicate a simple preference, as in, "I love pancakes!"

A LOVE THAT DEFIES DESCRIPTION

However, divine love is so awesome it defies description. There's no one definition that encompasses all the avenues love may take. And because love can't be neatly packaged, many pursue a myth rather than the love described in the Bible.

First John 4:7–8 helps us understand the true nature of God's love: "Beloved, let us love one another, for love is of God; and everyone who loves is born of

God and knows God. He who does not love does not know God, for God is love." John tells us two things: "love is of God" and "God is love."

Norman Grubb observed, "Love is exclusively a Person." What is love? Love is being filled with God. It's reflecting His Son, Jesus, in everything.

My awakening to God's love began during a serious illness while I was a student at Chicago's Moody Bible Institute. The school doctor urged immediate surgery for the removal of a tumor. Because the tumor appeared to be malignant, the operation was followed with radiotherapy. I shall always remember the honest concern of Dr. Titus Johnson, as he explained that my condition could be fatal, and, if not, the possibilities of my fathering children were remote.

During those anxious days, a Sunday school teacher sent me a booklet by James McConkey on the theme of God's love. As I read it, I saw my need to love God supremely and to allow His love to become my love. My sickness, the quietness of the hospital, the message of the booklet, and the possibility of an early death were all blended by the Great Physician to awaken my deep need of God's love. Through it all, I caught a vision of the love of God and the possibility of becoming an instrument of God's love to my world.

My hospital bed was my altar of sacrifice. I reminded the Lord of my desire to serve Him. I told Him that I wanted His will more than anything else in life. I prayed, "Lord, this hospital bed is my altar of sacrifice. If it pleases You, I'd like to be a *living* sacrifice. With Your help, I yield myself to You to become an instrument of Your love for others."

The result of that decision was life changing. And though I have further to go in becoming an instrument of God's love, that experience marked the beginning of my pursuit.

BECOMING A LOVE-FILLED PERSON

Let me suggest five steps in becoming a love-filled person.

Step One: Receive Personal Salvation. The apostle John teaches that God is the source of love. First John 4:7 reads, "Beloved, let us love one another, for love is of God; and everyone who loves is born of God and knows God."

All humanity, because of creation, can know a measure of God's love. Because of mankind's disobedience and sin, God's image in men and women was defaced, but not erased! However, we can still know and experience God's love. As 1 John 4:7 states, to be able to truly love, we must be born of God and know God.

Jesus said, "Unless one is born again, he cannot see the kingdom of God" (John 3:3).

The sacrificial death of Jesus on the cross is God's only remedy for sin. God, in His love, designed this plan of salvation so that we could be forgiven. When we understand that, our only reasonable response is to love and serve Him. John 1:12 reads, "As many as received Him, to them He gave the right to become children of God."

When we receive Jesus, we become the children of God! That's what the Bible says—*children of God!*

To become a person of God's love, one must know Jesus in a personal way. Love is not a law, nor a code, but *Jesus*. This is one of the most remarkable truths of Christianity. God knew we really couldn't love until we had experienced His love. So He expressed His love in the person of Jesus, so that we humans could grasp mercy, truth, grace, forgiveness, and joy—all of which are included in His perfect love.

Step Two: Pursue Love. Goals are important, and love is the most important goal. The apostle Paul urges each follower of Christ to "pursue love" (1 Corinthians 14:1). The word *pursue* speaks of a persistent search. It is the same word used to express Paul's relentless pursuit of the early Christians prior to his conversion to Jesus (Philippians 3:6). It is the word he used when he wrote, "I *press* toward the goal for the prize of the upward call of God in Christ Jesus" (Philippians 3:14, italics added). Paul is urging us to make God's love our relentless pursuit.

D. L. Moody tells how he did not fully understand the power of God's love until he heard Henry Moorhouse preach on John 3:16 for a full week. Richard Ellsworth Day, in his biography of Moody, *Bush Aglow*, records Moody's own account of what happened to him at those meetings: "I never knew up to that time that God loved us so much. This heart of mine began to thaw out; I could not keep back the tears. I just drank it in. . . . I tell you there is one thing that draws above everything else in the world and that is love.[1]

After this experience, Moody, who was already a successful Christian worker, saw for the first time the secret of a winsome church:

> The churches would soon be filled if outsiders could find that people in them loved them when they came in. This . . . draws sinners! We must win them to us first, then we can win them to Christ.

We must get the people to love us, and then turn them over to Christ.[2]

Yet Moody still felt restless until he began to experience the power of God's love in his life. His congregations showed signs of falling away. He found himself wondering if the gospel might need something added to it to make it attractive to people. While reading on a train from California, after attending a Sunday school convention, he recalled Henry Moorhouse saying to him four years earlier, "You are sailing on the wrong track. If you will change your course, and learn to preach God's words instead of your own, He will make you a great power."[3]

Moody realized then that he had been trying to explain what the Bible teaches rather than sharing its truths from an overflowing life. He had taken a course in reading, and when he selected a text and started to preach, he would immediately depart from it. Now, sitting on the train, Moody recalled with new understanding what an old gentleman in Boston had told him years before: "Young man, when you speak again, honor the Holy Spirit."[4]

That summer Moody made the rewarding commitment to give even his ignorance to Christ. New vitality flooded his life and ministry. Even the August heat did not keep the people away. Moody realized humbly that his sermons now had the evidence of God's power—power that had never been there before in the parade of his own knowledge.

At the close of his ministry at the Chicago Avenue Church, Moody's advice to his successor, Dr. Erdman, was, "Give the people the importance of God's love. If they're right here, they'll be right 95 percent of the time." God's love is a lifelong goal to be passionately pursued.

Step Three: Pray for God's Love. Paul prayed for God's love to be part of each Christian's life: "And this I pray, that your love may abound still more and more in knowledge and all discernment, that you may approve the things that are excellent, that you may be sincere and without offense till the day of Christ" (Philippians 1:9–10).

Start each day by praying that God's love will overflow in your life. Amy Carmichael, missionary to India, expressed this well in poetry:

Mender of broken reeds,
O patient Lover, 'Tis love my brother needs,
Make *me* a lover. That this poor reed may be

Mended and tuned for Thee, O Lord, of even me,
Make a true lover.[5]

Regularly, I pray this prayer for myself.

Step Four: Seek the Fruit of the Holy Spirit. Paul wrote, "The fruit of the Spirit is love, joy, peace, long-suffering, kindness, goodness, faithfulness, gentleness, self-control" (Galatians 5:22). Fruit comes slowly. It takes a seed, a flower, pollination, sunshine, rain, and contrary winds to produce the finished fruit. That's true in life too. Our lives are made up of sunshine and rain, blue skies and black, harsh winds, and pruning shears—all working to produce this special fruit of the Spirit.

In a lifetime of counseling people, I have observed that their goals generally can be reduced to love, joy, and peace. Isn't it interesting that these are included in the fruit of the Holy Spirit? Paul told the believers at Rome, "The love of God has been poured out in our hearts by the Holy Spirit who was given to us" (Romans 5:5).

Some people make the mistake of seeking the fruit of the Spirit without submitting to the Holy Spirit Himself. *The secret of the fullness of love is the fullness of the Holy Spirit.*

Scripture teaches that when we receive Jesus as Savior we actually become the dwelling place of the Holy Spirit. Paul asks, "Do you not know that you are the temple of God and that the Spirit of God dwells in you?" (1 Corinthians 3:16). This is a staggering fact. Think of it—God the Holy Spirit living in me—*all the time!*

In times past, God resided in the tabernacle and then in the temple. That was where He displayed His glory. Paul, however, reminds us that God now dwells in *us* (Colossians 1:27). The moment one receives Christ as Savior, that very moment the Holy Spirit comes to dwell within.

The word *dwell* in 1 Corinthians 3:16 has a beautiful depth of meaning. It means "to settle down" or "to stay permanently," as we do in our own homes. The Holy Spirit is a personal, permanent guest in our lives. The Holy Spirit is God in us *all the time.*

But we dare not take the Holy Spirit for granted. Paul warns, "Do not grieve the Holy Spirit of God, by whom you were sealed for the day of redemption" (Ephesians 4:30). G. Campbell Morgan asked, "How would you like to be compelled to live with somebody who was everlastingly grieving your heart by his conduct?" How badly we feel when we hurt someone we love! We would do anything to make amends for the disappointment and heartache we've caused. Just so, may we not grieve the indwelling Holy Spirit, who is the source of God's love in us. Rather, may we "be filled with the Spirit" (Ephesians 5:18).

Step Five: Love by Faith. We need to pray, "Lord, just as I received salvation by faith, so help me to love others . . . by faith."

Some people are harder to love than others. A twenty-two-year-old woman came to me for some guidance. As we talked, she poured out a tale of bitterness against her parents. After reading to her from the Bible, I was able to lead her to a personal faith in Jesus Christ as Lord and Savior. Almost immediately she said, "I want to be reconciled with my parents, but . . . how can I love them?"

"By faith," I gently answered. "Believe that God will give you His love for your parents."

How can you love? Think of someone who is difficult to love. Perhaps, you could make a list of that person's qualities. You might also ask yourself why he has those specific undesirable qualities. Then, in an act of genuine faith, resolve to love that person. Pray for him. Ask God to bless him. Seek to make a difference in his life.

Prayer for others has a boomerang effect: it benefits the one who prays. It was only when Job prayed for his miserable comforters that he was released from his own trouble. "The Lord restored Job's losses *when he prayed* for his friends" (Job 42:10, italics added). In fact, the Lord gave Job twice as much as he had before his affliction.

Just as we receive Jesus as Lord and Savior by faith, so we can love by faith as we allow God the Holy Spirit to shed God's love abroad in our hearts.

To look to ourselves and our shortcomings will only lead to failure. Jesus' disciples understood the hopelessness of living life in their own strength. They knew it was impossible, and so do we. But the good news is this: God knows it too! We are to look to Jesus Christ and His faithfulness.

God's perfect character stands behind His promises. His perfect love is available to fill us now. We need not struggle. We need only to allow God the Holy Spirit to pour out His love "in our hearts" (Romans 5:5).

QUESTIONS

1. What is the source of love and what is the first step in loving others?

2. Are goals important? List several verses that suggest Paul's goals.

3. Examine Paul's prayer in Philippians 1:9–11. What does this say about God's love?

4. What is the relationship of God's love to the work of the Holy Spirit?

NOTES

1. D. L. Moody, as quoted in Richard Ellsworth Day, *Bush Aglow* (Valley Forge, Pa.: Judson, 1936), 145.

2. Ibid., 146.

3. Ibid., 130.

4. Ibid., 131.

5. Frank Houghton, *Amy Carmichael of Donavhur* (Fort Washington, Pa.: Christian Literature Crusade, 1973), 224.

"Let brotherly love *continue*."

Hebrews 13:1 (ITALICS ADDED)

"Upon Jesus' authority, He gives the world the right to judge whether you and I are born again Christians on the basis of our observable love toward all Christians."

Francis Schaeffer, *The Mark of the Christian*

"And let us consider one another in order *to stir up love and good works*, not forsaking the assembling of ourselves together, . . . but exhorting one another, and so much the more as you see the Day approaching."

Hebrews 10:24–25

"The churches would soon be filled if outsiders could find that people in them loved them when they came in. This . . . draws sinners! We must win them to us first, then we can win them to Christ. We must get the people to love us, and then turn them over to Christ."

D. L. Moody, *Bush Aglow*

8

LOVING ONE ANOTHER THROUGH THE CHURCH

IN HIS BOOKLET *The Tyranny of the Urgent*, Charles E. Hummel tells how he was startled when someone said, "Your greatest danger is in letting the urgent things crowd out the important."[1]

Seeking to be a person of God's love never seems urgent, yet it is all-important. In fact, seeking to live out God's love is the highest pursuit for the Christian and the greatest need of the church.

The apostle Paul reminded the Corinthian Christians that loving God and loving people were their greatest calling. Paul said without this love, "I have become a noisy gong or a clanging cymbal" (1 Corinthians 13:1 NASB). Without this love, "I am nothing" (v. 2 NASB) and "it profits me nothing" (v. 3 NASB). Paul then calls this divine love, the "greatest" (v. 13 NASB).

A NEW COMMANDMENT

First Corinthians 13 is often called the love chapter of the Bible, but John 13 is also a great love chapter. Jesus said, "A new commandment I give to you, that you love one another; as I have loved you, that you also love one another. By this all will know that you are My disciples, if you have love for one another" (vv. 34–35).

Tradition tells of the farewell message of the aged apostle John to his first-century church. He urged them to love one another as he had often done before.

"We've heard that," they responded, "give us a new commandment." John paused and then deliberately said, "A new commandment I give to you, that you love one another." John had no other commandment that could equal loving one another. As far as he was concerned, everything in life is wrapped up in the bundle of love for God and love for fellow believers.

God's desire and will for the church is that its members "love one another." This is the reoccurring theme of the New Testament, as seen in the following verses:

> "Be kindly affectionate to one another with brotherly love" (Romans 12:10).

"Let brotherly love continue" (Hebrews 13:1).

"You shall love your neighbor as yourself" (James 2:8).

"Above all things have fervent love for one another" (1 Peter 4:8).

"Bearing with one another in love" (Ephesians 4:2).

"And this I pray, that your love may abound still more and more" (Philippians 1:9).

"Be encouraged, being knit together in love" (Colossians 2:2).

"May the Lord make you increase and abound in love to one another" (1 Thessalonians 3:12).

"Beloved, if God so loved us, we also ought to love one another" (1 John 4:11).

"Keep yourselves in the love of God" (Jude 21).

Tertullian, an early church leader, said: "It is our care of the helpless, our practice of loving-kindness that brands us in the eyes of our opponents. 'Look,' they say, 'how they love one another! Look how they are prepared to die for one another.'"[2]

Once we have received Jesus, we are urged and commanded to love one another.

A NEW MODEL

Often I am asked, "How can I communicate God's love in a self-centered world? Is it possible to be a love-filled person?"

Jesus modeled how to love. We're told to love as He loved. The question is asked, "But how did Jesus love?" He modeled love in two ways: by serving His disciples and the people around Him (Mark 10:45; John 13:1–17) and by sacrificing His life for the sins of the world (1 John 4:10).

Just before His death, Jesus, knowing who He was and why He had come into the world, took a towel "and began to wash the disciples' feet" (John 13:3–5). He showed love by serving others in the ordinary circumstances of life. Jesus was the number one leader of all time—and also the number one servant of all time. Jesus is the church's model for loving our world.

A NEW MARK

In the spring of 1970, the message of Francis Schaeffer broke upon the Christian world like refreshing rain. He reminded that decade that the vital mark of a believer is God's love. "By this all will know that you are My disciples, if you have love for one another" (John 13:35).

Through his classic work *The Mark of the Christian* (InterVarsity, 1970, 2006), Schaeffer continues to remind us that we will not be recognized as Jesus' disciples by our elaborate programs, extravagant facilities, elegant music, or eloquent preaching. Our distinguishing mark is not the shepherd's staff or the oxen's yoke, nor the fisherman's net. It is not even the familiar cross or crown. Our new mark is God's love. Peter, Paul, and John all agree that the way of God's love, is God's way for the church.

LOVING THE CHURCH

Personally, I could not continue the Christian life apart from the ministries of the local church. I need the love, instruction, encouragement, discipline, and accountability to the local church. I agree with the words of Timothy Dwight's hymn:

> I love Thy Church, O God!
> Her walls before Thee stand,
> Dear as the apple of Thine eye,
> And graven on Thy hands.[3]

For many years, I had the privilege of leading the Moody Bible Institute of Chicago, a parachurch organization and higher education institution. *Continually*, I urged each employee to keep close to the local church and to purposely avoid anything that in any way might detract from the local church. Jesus said, "I will build *My* church" (Matthew 16:18, italics added). Each local church is part of Christ's universal church and precious to Jesus.

The Holy Spirit uses many images to convey what the universal church is like. At times, the church is like a flock or a family. Occasionally, the church is pictured as a mighty army, or even a team. However, I want to call attention to the church as a building, a body, and a bride.

THE CHURCH AS A BUILDING

First, the church is like a building. Jesus said in Matthew 16:18, "On this rock I will build My church, and the gates of Hades shall not prevail against it." Do not misunderstand this. The church is not a building where believers meet to worship. It is rather a spiritual building made up of believers, with Jesus Himself as the "chief cornerstone" (Ephesians 2:19–22).

The church itself is the temple of God. It is the

dwelling place of His Spirit (see 1 Corinthians 3:16).

The Israelites in the wilderness were instructed by God to build the tabernacle, a movable place of worship. When it was completed, God Himself moved in. His visible glory, known as the *Shekinah*, rested there as a manifestation of His presence. All worship and sacrifices were made at the tabernacle, for that was the place of the presence of God.

Later, a permanent place of worship, the temple, was built. At its opening, it, too, was filled with the presence of God. His glory filled the place, again signifying that it was the dwelling place of God.

Once the church began, God no longer dwelt in man-made buildings. Paul told the Athenians, "God . . . does not dwell in temples made with hands" (Acts 17:24). The church is a "building" made without human hands. Paul described its construction in 1 Corinthians 3:10–11: "I have laid the foundation. . . . But let each one take heed how he builds on it. For no other foundation can anyone lay than that which is laid, which is Jesus Christ."

The first temple, the tabernacle, was made of cloth and animal skins. The second temple, the "house" Solomon built, was made of stones and cedar. But God's present temple, the church, is made up of people like you and me. It, too, should be a visible manifestation of the glory and presence of God. Unbelievers ought to be able to look at Christians and see in them a display of God's glory.

THE CHURCH AS A BODY

The church is also pictured in the New Testament as a body—the body of Christ. Colossians 1:18 says that Christ is "the head of the body, the church."

The Greek word in the New Testament for "church" is *ekklēsia;* the prefix *ek*, meaning "from" or "out," and the word *kaleō*, meaning "to call." The church is a group of believers in Jesus, called out from the world to be members of Christ's body. We are a living, growing, working body, with Jesus as our guide.

Just as our heads cannot be separated from our bodies without destroying the life, so it is with the church and Christ. The Head is inseparable from the body. We are partakers of the same life. We work together as a unit. We are vitally connected.

Like the physical body, the members are different but all special and necessary—functionally separate but interdependent. Each church member has an individual function, a gift that is unique, abilities that other Christians may not possess. But he or she is no less or more a member of the body than any other believer in Christ.

Do you see that? There's room for individuality in the body of Christ, yet we are all working toward the same goal. There are many differing kinds of ministries, but ultimately we all are of one mind.

Paul instructed the Corinthian Christians in the use of spiritual gifts. He pointed out that the Holy Spirit gives a multitude of gifts, "distributing to each one individually as He wills. For as the body is one and has many members, but all the members of that one body, being many, are one body, so also is Christ" (1 Corinthians 12:11–12).

Paul used that illustration to exhort the Corinthians to unity. "There should be no schism in the body, but . . . the members should have the same care for one another. And if one member suffers, all the members suffer with it; or if one member is honored, all the members rejoice with it" (vv. 25–26).

The responsibility of every church member is the same. We are to be united in purpose, mind, heart, goals, and love of one another. There is no room for pride or arrogance, and there's no room for an inferiority complex (vv. 14–21).

Each member of the body of Christ has unique

gifts and ministries, for that is the way the body functions best. The diversity lends itself to unity. No member is less necessary than any other. "Gifts were not intended to divide us; they were intended to expand our ability to multiply the work of Christ."[4] Spiritual gifts are given by the Holy Spirit according to His sovereign pleasure (v. 11).

As a member of the body of Christ, are you performing your function in harmony with the rest of the body? Do not try to be like someone else. Do not try to imitate the gifts of another member of the body. And do not fight against those who may differ slightly in function from you as long as you and they are united in purpose. Remember, diversity of function is just as important as unity of purpose.

How do we discover our spiritual gifts? By living a spirit-filled life and by observing how God uses us in the lives of one another.

THE CHURCH AS A BRIDE

The final picture of the church in the Scriptures is that of a bride. The church is the bride of Christ. In Ephesians 5, Paul deals with the correct relationship of a husband and wife. In verse 32, he ends his discussion by saying, "This is a great mystery, but I speak concerning Christ and the church."

Throughout the New Testament the church is portrayed as pure, like a bride arrayed in white, submissive and responsive to the love and leadership of Christ, the Bridegroom.

The marriage relationship is holy and, for that reason, is a picture of the relationship between Christ and His church. It's a permanent relationship, a relationship based on love, trust, and mutual submission and sacrifice. It is a relationship of unity based on common goals and commitment. But most of all, it is a relationship of purity.

As a *building*, the church is the dwelling place of God. That speaks of the importance of holiness. As a *body*, the church is an organism of which Christ is Head. That speaks of the importance of unity—the unity of all the members of the body of Christ. And as a *bride*, the church is married to Christ. That speaks of the importance of purity.

Holiness, unity, and purity—these are the qualities emphasized in these three great pictures of the church. And if the church is to succeed in her mission, it is precisely in these areas that she will succeed or fail.

Our challenge as individual members is to allow

the love of God to be "shed abroad in our hearts" (Romans 5:5 KJV). It is to exercise our gifts as strong, healthy, growing followers of Christ. If we do this, we will present to the world a convincing witness.

QUESTIONS

1. What is God's intention for His followers according to John 13:34–35?
2. How did Jesus model love for us?
3. What is the distinctive mark of a follower of Christ?
4. Suggest several images of the church in the Scriptures.
5. What are some of the spiritual gifts and how can we discover our gift?

NOTES

1. Charles E. Hummel, *The Tyranny of the Urgent* (Downers Grove, Ill.: InterVarsity, 1967), 4.

2. Tertullian, *Apologetics* 39.7

3. Timothy Dwight, "I Love Thy Kingdom, Lord," public domain.

4. Joseph Stowell, *Following Christ* (Grand Rapids: Zondervan, 1996), 173.

"And He gave some as apostles, and some as prophets, and some as evangelists, and some as pastors and teachers, for the equipping of the saints for the work of service, to the building up of the body of Christ."

EPHESIANS 4:11–12 (NASB).

"When a man loses the sacred significance of work and of himself as a worker, he soon loses the sacred meaning of time and of life."

CARL F. H. HENRY, *ASPECTS OF CHRISTIAN SOCIAL ETHICS*

"Jesus said to them, 'My Father is always at his work to this very day, and I, too, am working.'"

JOHN 5:17 (NIV).

9

CHRISTIAN SERVICE AND THE CHRISTIAN'S WORK

WHEN YOU HEAR the word *minister*, what pictures come to mind? If you're of English background, you probably think of the leaders in government. Most cabinet officers in the British government are called ministers. There's a prime minister, a defense minister, a minister of transport, and so on. There are junior ministers and senior ministers whose performance is judged on the basis of their ministerial ability.

While the government of the United States refers to its department heads as secretaries, it still retains the idea of ministry when it calls its appointed officials "civil servants" and its elected officials "public servants." The word *servant* is the same as *minister*.

For some, the word *minister* brings to mind "the head of a church." Perhaps you picture a minister standing in the pulpit teaching and preaching while the people listen.

The apostle Paul used the word *minister* in a third way. In Ephesians 4:11–12, he referred to the average lay person in the congregation as a minister. He thought of church leaders as equippers who prepare the people of the congregation for the work of ministry: "And He Himself gave some to be apostles, some prophets, some evangelists, and some pastors and teachers, for the equipping of the saints for the work of ministry, for the edifying of the body of Christ" (Ephesians 4:11–12).

A LIFE OF MINISTRY VERSUS
A LIFE OF SELF-SERVICE

According to Paul, the Christian life is a life of ministry. Individuals and churches grow in maturity only as they give themselves to serving others. The great commands of Jesus were not to love *ourselves* with all our heart, soul, and mind, but rather, to love *God* first and then others (Matthew 22:37–39). The priorities of the Christian life are God, others, and self.

The world's agenda is the opposite. The world begins by serving self, then others—and God is often forgotten. The world's service begins with the individual. Self is the primary consideration in everything.

During the Last Supper, Jesus shocked His disciples by washing their feet. He said to them, "You call Me Teacher and Lord, and you say well, for so I am. If I then, your Lord and Teacher, have washed your feet, you also ought to wash one another's feet. For I have given you an example, that you should do as I have done to you" (John 13:13–15).

Jesus was saying, "If I, the Son of God, am a servant, then for sure you must be servants also." When the mother of two of Jesus' disciples petitioned Him to give her sons a special place of honor in His kingdom, Jesus refused. "Whoever desires to become great among you, let him be your servant," He said. "And whoever desires to be first among you, let him be your slave—just as the Son of Man did not come to be served, but to serve, and to give His life a ransom for many" (Matthew 20:26–28). For Jesus, the way *down* is the way *up*. Greatness is achieved by service to others, not by power and prestige.

This truth is emphasized again in Philippians 2. The passage pictures the eternal Son of God, who set aside His rights as God, emptied Himself, and became a servant. The glory of His exaltation came not through ladder climbing, but through service. As followers of Jesus, we are to "let this [same] mind be in [us] which was also in Christ Jesus" (Philippians 2:5). George MacDonald once said, "God never gave man a thing to do concerning which it would be irreverent to ponder, . . . how the Son of God would have done it."[1] Jesus was the greatest servant of all history.

WHO PERFORMS THE SERVICE? THE CASE OF THE CONFUSING COMMAS

With the example of Jesus in mind, think carefully about Ephesians 4:11–12. It says God gave the church apostles, prophets, evangelists, and pastor-teachers, for (says verse 12 in the King James Version) the "perfecting of the saints (comma) for the work of the ministry (comma) for the edifying of the body of Christ."

I mention the commas because their placement creates confusion about the nature of the ministry. It's very possible to think, as many have, that verse 12 describes three responsibilities of the pastor-teacher: (1) to perfect the saints, (2) to do the ministry, and (3) to edify the body.

If this is how the passage is translated, we have a major problem on our hands. It implies a huge gap between the pastors, who do the work, and the people, who benefit from the work but basically sit there, as listeners only. It creates a dualism in the church by drawing a line between the clergy and the laity. The New Testament knows little of that distinction. The valid distinction is not between two *classes* of people in the church, but between two *functions*. Some people are equippers, and others, who have been trained by the equippers, are the ministers!

The *New American Standard* translation of Ephesians 4:11–12 makes this meaning clear. It says that God gave these officers, including pastor-teachers, "for the equipping of the saints (no comma) for the work of service (comma) to the building up of the body of Christ."

Perhaps you say to yourself, *Can one misplaced comma make all that difference?* Yes, it can! The one translation pictures a pastor doing all the work himself. It portrays the church as a one-man institution. But an accurate translation of the Greek pictures the pastor equipping the saints for the work of the ministry.

Imagine a basketball team where the coach tries to play all the positions himself! All his gifted players are left on the bench. When we rightly understand Ephesians 4:12, we see that the wise pastor is like a gifted coach. He equips the players to play. Instead of a one-man team, there is a full team.

Paul says that the pastor-teacher is to equip the believers. He is to minister the Word through preaching and teaching. The role of the saints is to take this training and do the work of the ministry.

Now the question arises: What kind of service ought Christians do? There are two answers. First, they must serve others in the world outside the church. Second, they must serve fellow believers within the church.

CHRISTIAN SERVICE IN THE WORLD

Because Jesus is our supreme example, it's important to ask, Where did Jesus serve? You'll remember that a large part of His life was spent with the people. Matthew 9:10 indicates that He often spent time with the outcasts of society. Why? As He said, "Those who are well have no need of a physician, but those who are sick" (v. 12).

Christ spent much of His time ministering outside the synagogue and temple to the oppressed of society. And so today our supreme task is to reach the multitude outside the church family. Christian fellowship is good, helpful, and even necessary. How-

ever, we dare not forget that we are calle
lost of our generation in Jesus' name. 7
is the Dead Sea because it receives and
The Dead Sea has no outlet. It receives only to keep.

Help someone in Jesus' name. Show some common courtesy in Jesus' name. Listen to someone's troubles in Jesus' name. Bear someone's burden in Jesus' name. The church is in the world to serve in Jesus' name.

CHRISTIAN SERVICE IN THE CHURCH

Jesus also served those who would be apostles of His church. He ministered to their needs. Sometimes He pulled them away from the crowds. Other times, He ministered to the crowds with them.

How does the Christian serve today in the body of Jesus Christ? Ephesians 4 suggests that it is the teaching of the Bible, the Word of God, that equips for ministry. Each of us needs to be linked to a body of believers where the Word of God is taught in practical clarity.

But *hearing* the Bible is not enough. We must also *do* the Word. One way we do the Word is by exercising the gifts that God has given us.

The Holy Spirit gives each Christian one or more

spiritual gifts, so that believers can serve others. Scripture offers several lists of these gifts. They're found in Romans 12; 1 Corinthians 12; Ephesians 4; and 1 Peter 4:10–11. There we see such gifts as apostleship, prophecy, evangelism, pastoring, teaching, helps, exhortation, giving, wisdom, knowledge, faith, hospitality, miracles, healing, discerning spirits, tongues, interpretation, and administration.

This list is not comprehensive. In fact, some of the gifts were primarily for the early church. But our great God has an inexhaustible supply of gifts for His people. Sometimes He gives several gifts to one individual. Sometimes He matches spiritual gifts with our natural talents. *But these gifts are given to the church for the purpose of serving.* When we neglect to exercise these gifts, the church is weakened. To learn which gift God has given you, study the Bible and pray. Ask the Lord to show you. Seek the counsel of mature believers who know you. If your church has seminars geared to finding out your spiritual gifts, participate in them. Often others can see your gift better than you can.

Occasionally, we hear economists talk about the dynamic of the free market. They say, "Allow people to buy and sell without the intervention of government and miracles will take place in the most unexpected ways and places." In an infinitely greater way, there's more dynamic in the body of Christ than in any free market. Christians are each endowed with unique Spirit-granted gifts. When Christians are free to develop their gifts, great things spontaneously occur.

Continued growth in the Christian life comes directly from joyful service. Death comes from selfishness. If you, as a Christian, will give yourself to serve as Jesus served, you will find yourself in the process. However, if you hold back, you will lose God's blessing.

Nothing cures loneliness like service in Jesus' name. Nothing disciplines wrong desires of the flesh like service. Nothing transforms inward insecurity like service. Service is another way we are to continue in the Christian life.

It's long past time that the world's idea of *success*, which has worked its way into the church, be replaced with God's idea of *service*.

THE CHRISTIAN'S WORK: AVOID THE EXTREMES

For a segment of society, work is pure drudgery, a sure sign of the original fall of mankind. Their attitude is negative and casual. They appear more interested in the coffee break and lunchtime than serious endeavor. "Thank God It's Friday" is their theme song, and the happy hour launches the long-awaited weekend.

At the other extreme are those who worship work. Their motto is "Thank God It's Monday." They have no qualms about working overtime. Work for them is an addiction. They pride themselves on being workaholics. They're not only motivated, they're so obsessed that marriage and children and health are sacrificed on the altar of work.

Between these extremes are many conscientious people who believe in the value of hard work, but whose voices are drowned out by the others. The workaholics get the headaches; and the ease-aholics, who live for the weekend, are quick to publish their own complaints.

Contrary to what many think, the Bible does not view work negatively, nor does it idolize work. The Bible talks about God's work, Adam's work, and even Jesus' work.

GOD'S WORK

An obvious fact from the first verse in the Bible is that God is a worker. "In the beginning God created the heavens and the earth" (Genesis 1:1). The text goes on to tell about each step of God's work: the expanse, the waters, the dry land, the vegetation, the animal life, and finally, the peak of God's initial work, the creation of man in His own image. Make no mistake about it, God's creation dignifies work.

We also see a picture of perfect job satisfaction. At the end of each stage of creation, the Lord God reflected on what he had accomplished and called it "good" (Genesis 1:4, 10, 12, 18, 21, 25). When He was finished, He assessed it in the superlative: "Then God saw everything that He had made, and indeed it was very good" (v. 31).

When the sixth day was over, God established the precedent of resting on the seventh day (Genesis 2:1–3). His pattern is to be our pattern. God is not a workaholic.

ADAM'S WORK

A second great fact of the Bible is that people were created to be workers. God is a worker, and we are to be workers. God created Adam and Eve to be His fellow workers. God plants the garden, and man tends it. "God blessed" Adam and Eve, saying, "Be fruitful and multiply; fill the earth, and subdue it; have dominion [rule] over the fish of the sea, over the birds of the air, and over every living thing that moves on the earth"; "tend [cultivate] and keep" the garden of Eden (Genesis 1:28; 2:15; see also 1:22). Work is elevated by God in these pre-fall commands.

There's no praise for idleness. God sends the rain and sun, but He expects man and woman to sow and reap. Luther said, "God milks the cows through you!" God's commands to Adam were not mere chores to be done. Rather, they were meant to underscore that work is good for us. It fulfills basic needs that God built into human beings. It brings satisfaction. It teaches responsibility. We were not meant to work in order to live, but rather to live in order to work.

What people seem to remember from the Bible about Adam and Eve's work is the curse of Genesis 3 —that women would experience pain in childbirth and that men would earn bread by the sweat of their faces. That picture, however, is of paradise lost, not a condemnation of work in general.

The command to work was never revoked. Even a brief look at the Fourth Commandment should remind us of that. We often think of it only as a command to rest, but there's more to it. "Remember the Sabbath day," it reads. Then it continues: "Six days you shall labor and do all your work" (Exodus 20:8–9). The legislation of creation has not been annulled by the fall. The command to work still stands.

JESUS' WORK

Perhaps the greatest approval of labor in the Bible comes when we view Jesus the worker. Mark 6:3 describes Jesus as a carpenter. We often forget that Jesus spent most of His life, until age thirty, working. His public ministry only lasted three years. Jesus was a skilled craftsman from a small town in Galilee. As a carpenter, He probably worked on homes, including roofs and doors and windows and stair fittings. Besides this, carpenters made couches, beds, chairs, tables, plows, yokes, and threshing equipment.

Strangely, after the childhood stories of Jesus, the Gospels do not mention His earthly father. Jesus is simply called "Mary's son." Jesus possibly learned His trade from Joseph. Probably Joseph died early, leaving Jesus, the oldest son, to carry on the family business and provide for His brothers and sisters. The pressures of work left little time for anything else.

The fact that Jesus, the eternal Son of God, spent the first thirty years of His life as a worker dignifies work. He said on one occasion, "My Father has been working until now, and I have been working" (John 5:17).

ABOUT OUR WORK

Having commented on God's work, Adam's work, and Jesus' work, it's time to say something about our work. What does our work have to do with continuing the Christian life? There are four basic concerns for every worker: *career, hours, pay,* and *boss.* Let's consider each briefly.

Studies suggest that the average adult changes *careers* at least twice before the age of sixty, although the exact amount remains uncertain.[2] Still, we should no longer think of a career as fixed. Nevertheless, choosing a career is a very important part of our working life.

In the Middle Ages there was a division between "sacred" and "secular" work. People saw the religious life as a higher calling. Many young people went off to the monastery or nunnery to escape a lower, worldly existence.

With the Reformation, teachers such as Luther and Calvin told the world that the division of work into higher and lower callings was unbiblical. Any useful and honorable line of work could be spiritual if it added to God's greater purpose of reconciling the world to Himself—whether it become planting or church planting.

Yet the old division between "higher" and "lower" types of work, or more popularly, between "full-time Christian work" and "secular work," persists. Some people mistakenly believe that there are few other careers open for Christians besides becoming a missionary or pastor. God does give special callings for such work, but those tasks are not for everyone.

In truth, *every* Christian who is a full-time Christian is in full-time Christian work. This is so whether he or she happens to serve hamburgers, teaches children, welds pipes, develops computer software, runs a business, or directs traffic.

All Christians are called to glorify God in *all* they do. Paul writes, "Whatever you do, do all to the glory of God" (1 Corinthians 10:31). A century ago, Gerard Manley Hopkins said: "It is not only prayer that gives God glory, but work. Smiting an anvil, sawing a beam, whitewashing a wall, driving horses, sweeping, scouring, everything gives God some glory if being in grace you do it as your duty."[3]

Of course, some lines of work do not bring God glory. Some occupations cause harm to people or offer little useful service to society. Some work lessens the integrity expected of a Christian. A good question to ask yourself is this: Could you see Jesus doing the same work in the thirty years before His public ministry? Is it honorable work?

FINDING THE RIGHT CAREER

How do you discover what career God wants you to pursue? Here are four suggestions. *First, know God.* Love Him with all your heart and love your neighbor as yourself. This is the number one calling of every Christian. *Second, know yourself.* Review what interests and gifts God has given to you. Identity and employment are closely related. Employment often grows out of our identity. *Third, know your options.* Evaluate which career opportunities are within your reach. *Fourth, know the mind of God.* You discern this by reading and obeying His Word and through prayer. As we do each of these, God will make our way clear.

Another concern of workers is their *hours*. A worker wants to know what particular job he has to do and how much time it will take. What principles should govern how we spend our time at work? If God directs us to a particular job, then our priority should be to do that job well.

GIVING THE BEST

Unfortunately, too many people stop looking for work once they find a job. They take advantage of the company benefits and scrimp on the work. If the employer gives us work, then we must fulfill our part of the bargain and do it well. That is part of the loyalty we owe our employer.

This is not a blind loyalty, for our first loyalty is always to God. Peter said, "We ought to obey God rather than men" (Acts 5:29). Paul told us to bring "every thought into captivity to the obedience of Christ" (2 Corinthians 10:5). In other words, we must evaluate what we do by the truth of Christ. Underneath this obligation comes the price of a day's work for a day's pay.

Of all people, Christians have the most reason to excel in their work. Quality work is never easy. It is never cheap. Nor is it accidental. It takes discipline and dedication, but if any people should abound in these qualities, it should be the followers of Jesus.

Perhaps you are surprised that I have not said anything about witnessing on the job. I have refrained until now because I'm skeptical of people who announce their faith before they prove it with their lives. The world is skeptical too. Bumper sticker Christianity is not very durable. The best witness I can have at work comes from the reputation of being a conscientious, honest, hard worker. With this kind of foundation, you will have plenty of opportunities to tell other people about the love of God in Christ.

WORK AND MONEY

Besides career and hours, an employee also is concerned about his *pay*. How much will he make? What will he do with it? It's good to remember that money is time plus energy plus personality. Money is an extension of ourselves. Like every other part of the Christian life, it must be dedicated to the Lord Jesus Christ.

Unfortunately, we often trivialize our work by our spending habits. We waste our money on such foolish things that we abuse the privilege of a good job with earning power. We belittle all the time and the energy that went into our work by our careless spending habits.

What should we do with our income? One thing is to provide for our families. First Timothy 5:8 says, "If anyone does not provide for his own, and especially for those of his household, he has denied the faith and is worse than an unbeliever."

An even greater priority is to give to the Lord in tithes and offerings. Proverbs 3:9 says, "Honor the Lord with your possessions, and with the firstfruits of all your increase." A tithe is a place to begin in giving.

Besides giving to the Lord and providing for our family, we are to give to those in need. Ephesians 4:28 tells us to work "that [we] may have something to give him who has need."

Our work enables us to give. Giving—not stock-piling—is a high calling of the Christian worker. Someone has said, "We make a living by what we get, but we make a life by what we give."[4] This is especially true of a growing Christian.

WHO'S THE BOSS?

A final concern of the worker is with his *boss*. A good boss or a bad boss makes a big difference. If you've ever had a boss who really wanted to help you grow in your job and who complimented you for good work, then you know what I'm talking about.

The Christian's ultimate boss is the Lord. In fact, Paul tells the Christian slaves in Ephesus to obey their masters as they would obey Jesus Christ. Most people work to please men, but Paul warned these slaves not to work to be seen. That is the cardinal vice of the workplace, and it's certain to sabotage quality. Rather, Paul said, in essence, "Go for the substance, not the image" (see Ephesians 6:5–8).

This should be a key difference between a Christian worker and a non-Christian. The Christian, working to please the Lord, should be more trustworthy and more committed to quality than anyone else.

I heard about a woman in a chocolate factory who was questioned by her friend. The friend said, "Tell me the difference your faith has made in regard to your work." She answered, "Formerly, I made chocolates for my boss. Now I make them for God." This illustration is simple, but it suggests the spirit we're talking about.

Carelessness and laziness should be far from us. The workplace is an arena where we continue our Christian life in word and in deed. This is what Paul was getting at in the book of Colossians when he gave important advice to the Christian workers. He wrote, "And whatever you do, do it heartily, as to the Lord and not to men, knowing that from the Lord you will receive the reward of the inheritance; for you serve the Lord Christ" (Colossians 3:23–24).

Here are some questions to ask yourself: Am I serving Jesus in the marketplace? Do I do my work as unto the Lord? Am I, by my work, a positive reflection of Jesus? Do I aim for quality? Am I a wise master builder, building with the right materials?

As Jesus reminded us, "The night is coming when no one can work" (John 9:4). Let's serve Him and others now.

QUESTIONS

1. How did Jesus exemplify Christian service?
2. Discuss Ephesians 4:11–12 and compare the *New American Standard Bible* with the King James Version. Why is the difference so important?
3. How can a Christian discover his or her spiritual gifts?
4. What about the Christian and employment? Suggest ways to pursue a career and discuss the kind of worker a Christian must be.

NOTES

1. George MacDonald, in *Draper's Book of Quotations for the Christian World*, comp. Edythe Draper (Wheaton: Tyndale, 1992), 348.

2. There are no definitive reports on the number of career changes, and the Bureau of Labor Statistics says clear criteria are needed for defining careers and career change. See Bureau of Labor Statistics, Frequently Asked Questions: "Does BLS have statistics on the number of times people change careers in their lives?" at http://www.bls.gov/nls/nlsfaqs.htm; and Carl Bialik, "Seven Careers in a Lifetime? Think Twice, Researchers Say," *Wall Street Journal*, September 4, 2010, at http://online.wsj.com/article/SB10001424052748704206804575468162805877990.html.

3. Gerard Manley Hopkins, in *Draper's Book of Quotations for the Christian World*, 653.

4. Sir Winston Churchill, in *Draper's Book of Quotations for the Christian World*, 235.

"But just as you excel in everything—
in faith, in speech, in knowledge,
in complete earnestness and in your love for us—
see that you also excel in the grace of giving."

2 CORINTHIANS 8:7 (NIV, ITALICS ADDED)

"Seldom repress a generous impulse."

GEORGE SWEETING

"Let each one give as he purposes in his heart,
not grudgingly or of necessity;
for God loves a cheerful giver."

2 CORINTHIANS 9:7

"God has given us two hands—one to receive with
and the other to give with. We are not citizens made
for hoarding; we are channels made for sharing."

BILLY GRAHAM, *THE QUOTABLE BILLY GRAHAM*

10

A GENEROUS IMPULSE

MY SCOTTISH parents occasionally reminded their children that when your *outgo* exceeds your *income*, then your *upkeep* is headed for a *downfall*.

They taught frugality regarding ourselves and generosity to God and others.

GOD'S NATURE ENCOURAGES A GENEROUS IMPULSE

The Old Testament speaks repeatedly of God's generosity. When God called Abraham, He promised to make his name great and prosper him with material goods. "Abram was very rich in livestock, in silver, and in gold" (Genesis 13:2). God also lavished His generosity on Isaac (Genesis 26:12–14), Jacob (32:13–21), Joseph (41:39–45), and Job (Job 1:1–3).

When Solomon became king of Israel, the Lord

appeared to him and said, "Ask! What shall I give you?" (1 Kings 3:5).

If God asked you that question, what would you answer? Your answer might reveal the real you, because God looks for a spirit of compassion and generosity.

Solomon answered, "Give to Your servant an understanding heart to judge Your people" (1 Kings 3:9). Because of Solomon's giving spirit, God responded with generosity. "I have given you a wise and understanding heart. . . . And I have *also* given you what you have not asked: both riches and honor, so that there shall not be anyone like you" (vv. 12–13, italics added). The word *also* affirms the generous nature of God.

David, the psalmist, gratefully wrote, "My cup runs over. Surely goodness and mercy shall follow me all the days of my life; and I will dwell in the house of the Lord forever" (Psalm 23:5–6). Our God is the God of the overflowing cup.

Jesus also spoke of God's generosity. "Give, and it will be given to you: good measure, pressed down, shaken together, and running over. . . . For with the same measure that you use, it will be measured back to you" (Luke 6:38).

A *measure* was a unit, like a pint, quart, or gallon. Some merchants were dishonest while others were stingy. They didn't give a "good measure." Jesus simply said, "The way you give is the way you will get."

The theme of generosity continues throughout the Bible. When the prodigal son of Luke 15 returns home, the father, who is a picture of the heavenly Father, *ran* to meet his repentant son, and announced, "Bring out the *best robe* . . . and put *a ring* on his hand and *sandals* on his feet. And bring the *fatted calf*" (vv. 22–23, italics added). The father gave the best robe . . . a ring . . . sandals . . . and a fatted calf!

When God gives joy, He gives *unspeakable* joy. When God gives peace, it's *peace that passes understanding.* His mercy is *limitless*, and His grace is *abundant.* When God gives, He gives His one and only Son. The cross of Jesus rises like a super plus sign—because God gives and gives and gives.

The poet asks:

"Must I be giving and giving again?"
My peevish and pitiless answer ran.
"Oh, no," said the angel, piercing me through.
"Just give 'til the Father stops giving to you."[1]

Billy Graham observed, "The key word of the self-ish, unregenerate person is *get*. The key word of the dedicated Christian should be *give*."[2] Richard Foster wrote, "God's great generosity to us sets us free to model that generosity to others. Because He gave, we are enabled to give."[3]

THE EARLY CHURCH MODELED A GENEROUS IMPULSE

The original church of the book of Acts faced gigantic needs because of its explosive growth. The numbers increased from twelve disciples to seventy, to one hundred twenty, then to three thousand, and finally five thousand souls (Acts 2:41; 4:4). To meet the staggering needs, "all who believed were together, and *had all things in common*, and sold their possessions and goods, and divided them among all, as anyone had need" (Acts 2:44–45, italics added).

Their generosity was so astonishing that Luke writes, "Nor was there anyone among them who lacked" (Acts 4:34). That's mind-expanding! Luke further elaborates, "All who were possessors of lands or houses sold them, and brought the proceeds of the things that were sold, and laid them at the apostles' feet; and they distributed to each as anyone had need"

(vv. 34–35). This speaks volumes concerning the generosity of the early Christians.

Later in the history of the early church, we're told how famine plagued the followers of Jesus in Judea, and how the Christians of Antioch came to their rescue. "Then the disciples, each according to his ability, determined to send relief to the brethren dwelling in Judea" (Acts 11:29). Paul added, "This they did, and sent it to the elders by the hands of Barnabas and Saul" (v. 30). Paul encouraged generous giving by telling the churches to whom the gift would be sent and by whom it would be sent. Assurance was given that their gift would be handled wisely and honestly.

Their giving was primarily to "the churches." He spoke of "the grace of God bestowed on the churches of Macedonia" (2 Corinthians 8:1).

Abundance was one of Paul's favorite words. He used it over sixty times in his letters to the churches and six times in 2 Corinthians 8 alone. Paul urges them to "abound in this grace also" (v. 7). Paul challenged the churches in Asia Minor and Ephesus to give a generous offering, not simply to relieve the distress of the poor believers in Jerusalem, but also to bring the churches the blessing that result from Christlike giving.

INCENTIVES FOR GIVING

What incentive did Paul give to the church regarding giving? He called attention first to *the giving of Jesus*, who left the wealth of heaven and the fellowship with God the Father to assume the poverty of sinners, that we might enjoy God's everlasting riches. Our primary motive for giving is the sacrifice of Jesus for sinners. (2 Corinthians 8:9). Jesus' atoning death for us is our number one reason for giving.

A second incentive for giving is the generosity of others. In this case, it was the Macedonian believers who gave *beyond* their ability (2 Corinthians 8:3). These Christians begged for the privilege of giving, even when they couldn't afford to give (v. 4). The generosity of other Christians is a powerful giving incentive. For the Macedonian churches, giving was a challenge, not a chore; an exciting blessing, not a burden. Giving was a sacred privilege to be sought, not something to be avoided.

HOW WE GIVE TO THE POOR

The question is not so much *whether* Christians should give to the poor, but *how* we can give to the poor. The principle of Jesus' ministry to the poor is that it must originate from a heart of genuine compassion. In His Sermon on the Mount, Jesus taught not only that helping the poor should be done ("when"—not if—"you do a charitable deed"; Matthew 6:2), but that it should be done without fanfare (6:1–4). Jesus regarded giving to the poor as the normal response of His followers.

But what was Christ's program for the poor? The Bible calls for a standard of justice for all, and beyond that, Jesus urged compassion and sharing which rises out of an awareness of human need.

In the Old Testament economy of God, poverty was not wiped out, but the poor were given special attention and protection. A poor worker was paid each day. If a poor man borrowed, giving his robe as security, the garment was to be returned before the owner needed it for warmth that night.

Persons who sold themselves as servants were freed each seventh year. If lands were sold, they could be redeemed by relatives. If not redeemed, they automatically reverted to their former owners every fifty years in the Year of Jubilee.

Anyone willing to work was assured of food to feed his family. It could be obtained by gleaning in fields, where produce was left deliberately for that purpose. The Old Testament book of Ruth describes how Ruth and her mother-in-law, Naomi, lived on such gleanings.

In New Testament times, the Jewish poor were less protected by laws. The duty of giving alms, however, was acknowledged and encouraged. Jesus often spoke of giving to the poor. The record of the early church is filled with references to Christian compassion for the poor, especially to fellow believers. Widows without support were cared for by the church, as seen in Acts 6:1 and 1 Timothy 5:9, 16. The poor were a subject of special concern at the first church council in Jerusalem. Paul mentions them in Galatians 2:10, where he writes that church leaders desired "that we should remember the poor." And then he adds, "The very thing which I also was eager to do."

Christians have always been God's special channel of generosity to the poor. However, we should also remember the fact that God blesses us—as we carry out this responsibility.

WHY WE SHOULD HELP THE POOR

Why should we help the poor? *First, the presence of the poor prompts us to exercise compassion.* How self-centered we become when we think only of ourselves! The presence of the poor is a constant reminder to be concerned about the needs of others.

Christians have been called out by God to demonstrate His love. The needs of our world are our primary concern. God's love is to be shown in tangible, practical ways. John writes in 1 John 3:17–18, "But whoever has this world's goods . . . and shuts up his heart from him, how does the love of God abide in him? . . . Let us not love in word or in tongue, but in deed and in truth." John is speaking here of love for fellow Christians. But Christian love reaches beyond the confines of our own church family.

So Paul wrote the church in Thessalonica, "The Lord make you increase and abound in love to one another and to all" (1 Thessalonians 3:12). As the church ministers to the poor, inside its membership or outside, it demonstrates God's love in a tangible, practical way.

Jesus taught that the *will of God* can be summed up in the two great commandments—love God and love your neighbor. If we would do the will of God in our day, we must have compassion on the poor.

Second, the presence of the poor gives us opportunity to prove that Christ has changed our lives and made them new. Helping the poor, especially when it costs us time and money, is not a natural instinct.

Instead, our old sin nature is inclined to look the other way. Compassion, on the other hand, is a clear evidence of the inner work of God the Holy Spirit.

The apostle James speaks of faith and works. Real faith produces works (James 1:22–25). Our acts are proof of faith. The Christian who genuinely helps the poor proves beyond the shadow of a doubt that he shares the life of Jesus Christ.

Third, the poor give Christians opportunity to lay up heavenly treasure. "He who has pity on the poor lends to the Lord," says Proverbs 19:17. "And He will pay back what he has given." To give to the poor for Jesus' sake is to invest money in heaven. Not only is such treasure safe from moth and rust, but it helps our minds and hearts to be fixed on heaven as well. "For where your treasure is," Jesus said, "there your heart will be also" (Matthew 6:21). It is not just a duty for the Christian to help the poor. In the wisdom of God, helping the poor is an exciting opportunity that encourages our spiritual growth.

There's a practical side to helping the poor. How should a church reach out? The first concern of any church is for the poor among its members. Does some fellow Christian struggle under the burden of inadequate housing? Has sickness brought financial stress?

The church can help in such a situation. Are children in need of clothing? Is someone out of work? The church should be concerned. Many churches have special funds for providing material help. Often these can be used to relieve a difficult situation.

But individual Christians also have an obligation. If I see a need within my power to meet, I dare not turn away. God will help me, if I share in love and trust, and will meet my needs as I give generously to others.

We must not turn our backs on the needs of the world. The apostle James warns, "If a brother or sister is naked and destitute of daily food, and one of you says to them, 'Depart in peace, be warmed and filled,' but you do not give them the things which are needed for the body, what does it profit?" (James 2:15–16).

That cannot be the outlook of the Christian. The Christian is to love, care, and show compassion, even at the cost of significant sacrifice.

Could there be someone in your church who needs more or better food? Someone who needs to see the dentist or be fitted with glasses? Does some family need warmer winter outfits for their children? It could well be your personal opportunity to minister and perhaps your chance to receive a blessing.

The same principles hold for those we encounter outside the circle of church membership. If we see a need and it lies within our ability to be of help, we have a responsibility to help. The person involved may be a neighbor down the street. Or we may share in some united effort to help the disadvantaged in a worthy way. Neither the church as a body nor individual Christians can turn away from need, wherever it may be.

And then there is the yawning chasm of world-wide need. The church as a whole, and every member of the church, can have part in helping somewhere in our world. The need is so great that it's impossible to respond to every need, but we can help generously with some. Jesus told his disciples, "Freely you have received, freely give" (Matthew 10:8). Our first and greatest obligation, of course, is to share the eternal Bread of Life. But we cannot withhold the bread of material help when it lies within our power to give it.

TWO PARABLES ON HELPING THE POOR

Jesus told two parables that may help us see our obligation. The first, recorded in Luke 16, was about a rich man and a beggar. The rich man, Jesus said, lived out his life in luxury. In time he died and perished—

not merely because he had been rich, of course, but because he had been satisfied with riches and had looked no further. The poor man had lived out his life unnoticed at the rich man's very doorstep.

The parable teaches the folly of trusting riches, but it also reminds us that the poor are all around. Like the rich man, *we can shut them out, or, like Jesus, we can help them out.*

The other parable is the story of the Good Samaritan (Luke 10:25-37). Three travelers in succession saw a man in a desperate plight. He had been robbed, beaten, and left beside the road to die. Two of the men who passed by the victim professed to be religious. But they did not want to get involved. The third, a Samaritan, took the time and trouble to help. He bound up the wounds of the injured man and took him to a place of safety. He even arranged to pay his bills until the victim was back on his feet.

The church collectively and Christians individually have been called to be generous neighbors. We cannot prevent the tragedies of life that leave poor people by the wayside. Nor can we help everyone. But we can help many who are within our reach.

Remember the two kinds of attitudes—the rich man lived a lifetime indifferent to the beggar at his doorstep; the Samaritan in a moment of opportunity chose to make himself a blessing. God calls you and me to be generous, like the Good Samaritan. We need to be willing to share not only the good news of salvation, but also we need to share in the material needs of those around us.

John Wesley had a famous saying: "Get all you can, save all you can, give all you can." Dallas Willard suggests a modification: "Get all you can; save all you can; freely use all you can within a properly disciplined spiritual life, and control all you can for the good of humankind and God's glory. Giving all you can would then naturally be a part of an overall wise stewardship."[4]

Seldom repress a generous impulse, because giving is godlike. Generous giving is an essential part of our growth, as we continue the Christian life.

QUESTIONS

1. Give a biblical illustration of the generous nature of God.
2. How did the early church respond to the needs of fellow believers? Give several examples.
3. What incentives did Paul give to the churches of Macedonia for giving? (2 Corinthians 8:1–2, 9)
4. Discuss several reasons for helping the poor.

NOTES

1. Anonymous, number 10728 in *Draper's Book of Quotations for the Christian World*, comp. Edythe Draper (Wheaton: Tyndale, 1992), 587.

2. Billy Graham in *The Quotable Billy Graham*; Cort R. Flint, ed. (Anderson, S.C.: Drake, 1966), 80.

3. R. J. Foster, *Freedom of Simplicity* (New York: Harper, 1981), 30.

4. Dallas Willard, *The Spirit of the Disciplines* (New York: HarperCollins, 1988), 217.

"Therefore do not be unwise,
but *understand what the will of the Lord is.*"

Ephesians 5:17 (italics added)

"Not as I will, but as You will. To be able to say those
words and truly mean them is the highest point we
can ever hope to attain. Indeed, we have broken
out of time's hard shell to breathe, not its stale air,
but the fresh exhilarating air of eternity."

Malcolm Muggeridge,
Quotations for the Christian World

"The God of our fathers has appointed you to know
His will and to see the Righteous One and to hear an
utterance from His mouth. For you will be a witness
for Him to all men of what you have seen and heard."

Acts 22:14–15 (nasb)

"To walk out of His will is to walk into our own."

C. S. Lewis, *Perelandra*

11

HOW TO KNOW THE WILL OF GOD

TO CONTINUE the Christian life requires an awareness and submission to the will of God. I can't imagine any follower of Jesus being disinterested in God's will for their life.

Repeatedly, the Bible tells us of God's desires for His children. Those that He accomplishes are called "God's will." Paul wrote to the believers in Ephesus: "He made known to us the mystery of his will according to his good pleasure, which he purposed in Christ (Ephesians 1:9 NIV).

Knowing and doing God's will is implied throughout Scripture. "Whoever does the will of My Father in heaven is My brother and sister and mother" (Matthew 12:50).

Divine guidance is promised throughout the Bible. "I will instruct you and teach you in the way you should go; I will guide you with My eye" (Psalm 32:8; see also Isaiah 58:11; Proverbs 3:5–6; John 8:12).

The overwhelming message of Scripture is that God has a plan for those who follow Him (Psalm 37:23). This means that there's hope for each believer in Jesus. Yes, God has a plan for each of His children.

THE BIBLE AND GOD'S WILL

The will of God and the Word of God are inseparable. The Bible is our guidebook for Christian growth. Nowhere else can we find a more complete picture of God's will for our lives. This is true in terms of general principles and it is true in terms of specific guidance. Much of God's will for you as an individual has already been given in the Bible. You may not know what it is, but that's possibly because you have not taken the time to search for it in the Bible. Paul praised the believers in the city of Berea because "they received the message with great eagerness, and examined the Scriptures every day" (Acts 17:11 NIV).

Throughout the Bible there are literally hundreds of instructions about God's desires that address many of the decisions we face in life. Whenever there is a matter of uncertainty in our minds, whenever we need to have answers from the Lord, our first question should be, Does the Bible have anything to say about this?

We can be sure that God's will for our lives will never contradict what He has already revealed in His written Word, the Bible.

God's will for us today is always in harmony with what God has given in the Bible.

Robbery, adultery, and murder are always wrong. We also know that fathers are not to provoke their children, but rather to "bring them up in the training and admonition of the Lord" (Ephesians 6:4). Likewise, the followers of Jesus are not to be drunk with wine, but to "be filled with the Spirit" (Ephesians 5:18). When Jesus was asked what the greatest command of Scripture was, He said "'Love the Lord your God with all your heart, and with all your soul, and with all your mind.' This is the first and great commandment. And the second is like it: 'Love your neighbor as yourself.' On these two commandments hang all the Law and the Prophets" (Matthew 22:37–40).

Three times in the gospel of John, Jesus specifically commanded that we love one another. "A new command I give you: Love one another. As I have loved you, so you must love one another" (John 13:34 NIV). "My command is this: Love each other as I have loved you" (John 15:12 NIV). "This is my command: Love each other" (John 15:17 NIV). This instruction is repeated in Romans, 1 Thessalonians, 1 Peter, 1 John (five times), and 2 John (see also Hebrews 10:24; 13:1; James 2:8). Love for fellow Christians is not an option for followers of Jesus.

Living in harmony with others and being free of anger is the standard for believers. "If it is possible, as far as it depends on you, live at peace with everyone," the apostle Paul said. "Do not take revenge, my friends, but leave room for God's wrath, for it is written: 'It is mine to avenge; I will repay,' says the Lord" (Romans 12:18–19 NIV).

Put aside "hatred, discord, jealousy, fits of rage, selfish ambition, dissensions, factions" (Galatians 5:20 NIV). "'In your anger do not sin': Do not let the sun go down while you are still angry" (Ephesians 4:26 NIV). "Get rid of all bitterness, rage and anger, brawling and slander, along with every form of malice" (Ephesians 4:31 NIV). Again, these are not options for the Christian.

A direct command is a clear way in which God speaks His will. But what about the areas in which the Bible is not clear or appears to be silent—where there are no direct commands or specific teaching? At such times we must rely on God's promises, follow biblical principles, and depend on the guidance of the Holy Spirit.

David had this assurance from God: "I will instruct you and teach you in the way you should go; I will guide you with My eye" (Psalm 32:8). God has promised that as believers trust in Him, He will show them the way they should go. He will reveal His will. Solomon's words in Proverbs are helpful: "Trust in the Lord with all your heart, and lean not on your own understanding; in all your ways acknowledge Him, and He shall direct your paths" (3:5–6).

Philippians 2:13 reminds us that God "works in you both to will and to do for His good pleasure." In other words, God will do His part in communicating His will to us. First Corinthians 2:15–16 tells us that God has given us the mind of Christ. This means that a spiritual person has the God-given discernment to make the right decisions.

In an article entitled "Four Ways to Find God's Will," A. W. Tozer writes:

On the surface it might appear more spiritual to seek God's leading than just to go ahead and do the obvious thing. But it isn't. . . . Except for those things that are specifically commanded or forbidden in the Scriptures, it is God's will that we be free to exercise our own intelligent choice. . . . In almost everything that touches our everyday life on earth, God is pleased when we're pleased. He wills that we be as free as birds to soar and sing our Maker's praise without anxiety. God's choice for us may not be only *one* but rather any one of a score of possible choices. The man or woman who is *wholly and joyously surrendered to Christ* can't make a wrong choice—any choice will be the right one.[1]

The Christian life is not like receiving a lifelong blueprint from heaven. It is rather a day-by-day walk with God. Although God is able to direct you all at once into some life's work, it's more likely that He will lead you a step at a time. It has been said that the way to see far ahead in the will of God, is to go ahead just as far as you can see. That's the key, a step-by-step walk with God.

It is very important to properly interpret God's Word. Paul told Timothy, his son in the faith, "Be diligent to present yourself approved to God, a worker who does not need to be ashamed, rightly dividing the word of truth" (2 Timothy 2:15).

Some Christians treat the Bible lightly. They claim verses without regard to the context. This is unwise and hurtful. In his book *God's Will for Your Life*, S. Maxwell Coder noted, "There is no doubt that God has often brought a certain verse to the attention of one of His children in an unusual and almost miraculous manner, for a special need, but the Word was never intended to be consulted in a superstitious manner."[2]

Another principle to remember is that guidance that has to be forced out of the Bible is really no guidance at all. God will seldom reveal His will to us if we try to force truth from His Word. Too many people fail to realize that a proper interpretation of the Bible requires that we first study a passage in its proper context and then compare various passages to get a complete picture of God's principles. Lifting verses out of context and tailoring them to suit a particular need may bring an answer, but it will not be the right answer.

In the booklet *Getting to Know the Will of God*, Alan Redpath describes how he sought to determine if God would have him enter the ministry. He made a list of all the arguments in favor of his staying in business. Each morning as he spent time in personal Bible study, he asked the Lord to show him particular verses that would counter each of the arguments he had written down.

"Lord, I am not here to evade You," Redpath prayed. "I am here because I want to know Your will. You saved me in order to guide me. Very well, then, Lord, what is Your will?"

Redpath explained what happened next:

Day by day I turned to my Bible. Almost every day a verse seemed to speak to me and I began to write that verse against one of the arguments. At the end of a year, every argument in favor of staying in business had been wiped out. It took over a year, but I was not in a hurry. I was willing to wait; I wanted it to be in God's time. Too much was at stake to dash into the thing. I wanted to intelligently find the will of God. And I found it as I sought the Lord through my daily reading and meditation. I committed it all to the Lord and step by step, the way opened.[3]

Do you want to know God's will? Then search for it first in the Bible. The psalmist wrote, "The entrance of Your words gives light" (Psalm 119:130). You can have God's light shining in your life, if you will obey His written Word.

PRAYER AND THE WILL OF GOD

Another means of guidance in the will of God is prayer. In His Word, God speaks to us. When we pray, we are talking to God. Communication is never possible unless there are two parties involved. Constant communication with our heavenly Father is vital if we truly want to know His plan for our lives. Someone has said, "Nothing lies beyond the reach of prayer except that which lies *outside* the will of God." As we study the Bible and as we study the history of the church, we find that those men and women who truly accomplished great things for God were those who spent much time *with* God in prayer.

As a college student, Paul Little heard a speaker ask a question that changed his life. "How many of you who are concerned about the will of God," asked the man, "spend five minutes a day asking Him to show you His will?"

"It was," says Little, "as if somebody had grabbed me by the throat. At that time, I was . . . concerned about what I should do when I graduated from the university. I was running around campus, going to this meeting, reading that book trying to find some-body's little formula . . . I was frustrated out of my mind, trying to figure out the will of God. I was doing everything but getting into the presence of God and asking Him to show me."[4]

What about you, friend? Are you concerned enough to spend as little as five minutes a day in prayer to ask God to show you His will? It is notable that after the apostle Paul's conversion on the road to Damascus, his first words were, "Lord, what do You want me to do?" (Acts 9:6). Knowing God's will was his greatest pursuit. He wanted God's will more than life itself. Nothing should be allowed into our daily schedule that will crowd out our time alone with God.

I know a great deal about my wife's interests. I know her likes and dislikes. I know what her favorite foods are, what kinds of books she likes to read, all about her. Why? Because I have spent many years in close communication with her. I have come to know her in an intimate and beautiful way. The closer we commune with our heavenly Father, the better we are going to know Him. The more time we spend in His presence, the less trouble we will have in determining His will. Prayer is a vital means of guidance into the will of God!

THE HOLY SPIRIT AND GOD'S WILL

Closely related to the upward ministry of prayer is the inward working of the Holy Spirit. Jesus told His disciples that when the Comforter, or the Holy Spirit, would come, He would guide them into all truth. One of the primary works of the Spirit in the Christian's life is to give wisdom and discernment—to demonstrate God's will. Paul declared, "For as many as are led by the Spirit of God, these are sons of God" (Romans 8:14). To the church at Philippi he wrote, "It is God who works in you both to will and to do for His good pleasure" (Philippians 2:13). God's Spirit is able to bring about the miraculous working of His will in our lives, but we must be willing to let Him have complete control and to be filled with the Spirit (Ephesians 5:18).

How does the Holy Spirit bring guidance in the Christian's life? Usually He does so by an inward urging or compelling. In the book of Acts we find specific references to this compelling power. While Philip was busily engaged in a successful evangelistic effort, the Holy Spirit spoke to him and said, "Arise and go toward the south . . . to Gaza" (Acts 8:26). He was compelled to minister specifically to an Ethiopian who was hungry for God.

Peter was led by the Spirit to take the gospel of Christ to the house of Cornelius.

Paul was directed by the Spirit to witness to the Macedonians. Hundreds of examples are given in God's Word of men who were directed by God's Spirit in specific ways. To the child of God, the voice of the Holy Spirit can be just as clear and plain as if it were audible.

GOD'S WILL AND THE
NORMAL CIRCUMSTANCES OF LIFE

Guidance in the will of God often comes to us in the normal circumstances of life. F. B. Meyer, the great English preacher, said: "God's impressions within and His Word without are often corroborated by His Providence around, and we should wait quietly until these three focus into one point."[5]

The most obvious facts of life can help us determine what God has and what He does not have for us. If, for instance, you find it difficult to carry even a simple tune, it is unlikely that God would have you sing solos in your church! Gifts, abilities, aptitude— all are given to us to help us determine what our life's work should be.

But circumstances and the obvious facts of life

should not be given more consideration than they deserve. Too often Christians become confused in their search for God's will because they make circumstances the primary factor in the decisions they make. God in His providence will place any number of steppingstones in our path. He will use the counsel and advice of friends and relatives. But He still expects us to be dependent upon Him.

Do you want to know God's will? Then be very sure that your life is acceptable to God. Be careful to meditate in God's Word daily and to spend time in prayer. Be sensitive to the inward voice of the Holy Spirit and to the everyday experiences God brings your way.

SALVATION IS WHERE WE BEGIN

God is sovereign and can do anything He chooses to do. However, for the most part, He chooses to acknowledge those who acknowledge Him as Lord and Savior. Personal faith in Jesus Christ is essential in understanding the will of God. The apostle Peter reminds us that God is "not willing that any should perish but that all should come to repentance" (2 Peter 3:9).

When I repented of my sins and by faith turned

from myself to Jesus as my Lord and Savior, I become a child of God (John 1:12–13). As a child of God, I have the privilege as well as the authority to come to my Heavenly Father for guidance.

In his book *The Perfect Will of God*, G. Christian Weiss asks:

> Can you think of a father who has no will or plan for the life of his son? Can you imagine a mother who has no clear will or definite ambition for her daughter? Can you imagine a man who has no special desire or pattern in the one he chooses to be his wife? . . . A captain who has no plan for his soldiery? An employer who has no plan or pattern to guide the labor of his workers? If so, then you may also think that God does not have a plan for your life, for every one of these symbols is used in the Bible to represent the relation the Christian bears to his Lord.[6]

If you are unsure of your relationship to Jesus Christ, I urge you to humbly call upon Him in prayer. Perhaps this prayer might express how you think and feel:

Dear Lord, I understand that I have been going in the wrong direction, away from Your will. I now ask that You turn me around.

I believe that You are the only one who can do this. I repent of everything that I have done that has displeased You. I believe that Jesus died on the cross for my sins. I ask forgiveness for my sins. Receive me into Your family, and give me the gift of eternal life. From today forward, take over as my Lord and Savior. I sincerely want to do the will of God. In Jesus' name, Amen.

A SURRENDERED LIFE

Early in my Christian life, I heard someone say, "The condition of an enlightened mind is a surrendered heart." That helped me to affirm God's will for my life.

The apostle Paul calls upon each follower of Christ to "present" his body "a living sacrifice, holy, acceptable to God, which is [his] reasonable service" (Romans 12:1). The central verb in this text is *present*, or *offer up*. Marion Nelson wrote:

This word was commonly used to refer to the act where the owner of the sacrificial victim gives up his victim to the priest for use in the Jewish worship service. Paul urges every Christian, as a believer-priest (1 Peter 2:9; Revelation 1:6) to offer his entire person, including his body and mind, to God for the purpose of service. Once offered, God accepts, and from then on the person is obligated to perform whatever service or duty is asked by God. Also, from then on God is obligated to deal in a disciplinary manner with that person if he shirks his duty.[7]

If you are to understand the "good and acceptable and perfect will of God" (Romans 12:2), you will want to make a positive presentation of your life to God. To present your body as a living sacrifice means to be in full compliance with God's will. It means to place yourself upon God's altar. It means to affirm His purposes for your life.

The story is told of the great composer Felix Mendelssohn visiting a German cathedral to see a new organ. At that point in his life, his music was well known but he was not. When he arrived at the cathedral, he found a young organist practicing. It so happened that the young man was playing one of Mendelssohn's own pieces. Mendelssohn walked up to the organist and, without introducing himself, requested to play the new instrument. The young organist refused, saying that he did not allow any strange hands to touch this keyboard.

Mendelssohn lingered for a moment and then wandered about the sanctuary. Soon he returned and asked, "My friend, will you allow me to play just a little?"

The young organist was angered and asked Mendelssohn to leave the building, saying, "No inexperienced hands dare touch the keyboard of this new organ."

Again, Mendelssohn retreated and even left the sanctuary. But try as he would, he could not go away. His soul was aflame with desire, and he yearned for an opportunity to play the new instrument. For the third time, he returned and said, "My friend, excuse me, but I feel I must ask you once again. Please let me sit down and play the organ, just a little."

Exasperated by Mendelssohn's persistence, the young organist consented to let him play. Mendelssohn then sat down and began adjusting the instrument to suit him, while the organist started to leave the sanctuary. As soon as Mendelssohn began to play, the young man rushed back to the organ. Looking earnestly at the composer, he asked, "Tell me, sir, who are you?"

"My name is Mendelssohn."

"Oh, forgive me!" the young organist exclaimed. "I didn't know who you were. Just think, I wouldn't let the master musician take my place and play my instrument!"

We're not very skilled at playing the keyboard of life. God, however, never intended for any of us to live life alone. The triune God—God the Father, God the Son, and God the Holy Spirit—gently invites us to allow Him to guide our lives. He lovingly calls out, "Let me touch the keyboard, and make music in your life."

SINCERITY AND GOD'S WILL

To know God's will requires more than intellectual curiosity. It requires a sincere, seeking heart. John 7:17 has always intrigued me: "If anyone wills to do His will, he shall know concerning the doctrine, whether it is from God."

Some people, rather than sincerely seeking God's will, simply want His approval of their personal agenda. I question whether God reveals the fullness of His will to those who merely play with it.

J. Sidlow Baxter tells of a young Christian woman who was infatuated with a young man who was not a believer. The girl's friends were concerned about the relationship, and did their best to warn her. They attempted to show her the teaching of Scripture concerning an unequal yoke (2 Corinthians 6:14), but the more they talked, the more determined she became. Finally, they persuaded her to pray together about the situation. With emotional gulps, she prayed, "Lord, Thy will be done, but please let me have Jimmie!"[8]

God will never lead us to do anything that is contrary to His written Word. Unless we're willing to do what He has told us, we're wasting time searching for further guidance. We must seek God's will with a sincere heart.

SEPARATION AND GOD'S WILL

God's will can be discovered better and understood better by those with clean hearts, clean hands, and clean motives. Paul teaches this in 1 Thessalonians 4:3, 7. He writes, "This is the will of God, your sanctification: that you should abstain from sexual immorality. . . . For God did not call us to uncleanness, but in holiness."

The word *sanctify* means two things: "to cleanse" and "to set apart." It is the will of God that we be clean and set apart for His glory.

We are set apart to God, in one sense, the moment we put our faith in Jesus, for we are bought with the price of His blood. Some day we shall be set apart from sin forever, by being taken to glory with Him. But 1 Thessalonians 4:3 speaks of our present responsibility.[9]

In 1 Thessalonians 4:3, we're told to "abstain from sexual immorality." The word *abstain* means "stay away from." How far away? Far enough away to remain pure. God expects that, as His temple, His abiding place, our bodies will be clean. God designed sex, and it is good and beautiful when used as He designed it—for the marriage relationship. In verse 4 Paul adds, "Each of you should know how to possess his own vessel in sanctification and honor." According to the context, it seems that Paul is speaking about the body. He says, "Control your body."

Paul goes on to say, "No one should take advantage of and defraud his brother in this matter, because the Lord is the avenger of all such, as we also forewarned you and testified. For God did not call us to uncleanness, but in holiness" (1 Thessalonians 4:6–7). Sexual immorality is an act of fraud. It cheats people, robbing them of the joy and purity God intended for sex.

Obviously, there is no way that we can remove all the sexual influences of the world around us. Nor are we supposed to isolate ourselves from this present world. The Bible says that though we are in the world, we are not *of* the world (John 17:15–16). We are not to pursue the world's agenda. We are to be separated to God for His glory.

IS IT POSSIBLE TO MISS GOD'S WILL?

Finally, is it possible to miss God's will for your life? Yes, it is, though all need not be lost.

Jonah missed God's will. However, he was given a second opportunity (Jonah 3:1), which he seized so that he experienced unprecedented blessing.

Abraham, also, instead of going immediately to the Promised Land, settled in Haran. However, God gave Abraham another chance, and he responded in obedience (Genesis 12:5). Moses, too, failed greatly (Acts 7:20–25) but was recommissioned at the age of eighty (Exodus 3:10). God not only gives a second chance, but often gives a third and fourth chance.

John Mark, a helper of Paul, fled the difficulties of ministry but was given another chance (2 Timothy 4:11). He even had the privilege of writing the gospel of Mark.

Peter failed greatly but was restored to significant usefulness.

If you have failed, all is not lost. The point is to seek God's forgiveness and begin to do His will from this moment forward. Granted, there are consequences because of neglect or disobedience regarding the past, but we may learn from our failures and renew our commitment to do the will of God.

It is a major mistake to look back thinking of what you might have been or done. Instead, use the days and weeks before you, even if they are few, to do the will of God to the best of your ability.

ESSENTIAL ELEMENTS IN KNOWING GOD'S WILL

Do you want to know the will of God? These elements are essential:

1. Read and study the Bible.
2. Pray for God's guidance.
3. Be sensitive to the work of the Holy Spirit.
4. Be alert to normal circumstances.
5. Be sure that you are truly saved.
6. Surrender yourself to God.
7. Sincerely commit your desires to Jesus Christ.

8. Separate yourself to God for His glory.

If you are right in these areas, then do anything you want to do. You say, "What do you mean?" I mean, "Do anything you want to do—for if you are right in these eight areas, you will want only the glory of God." Psalm 37:4 affirms this: "Delight yourself also in the Lord, and He shall give you the desires of your heart."

The growing Christian lives in the spirit of "Your will be done on earth as it is in heaven" (Matthew 6:10).

QUESTIONS

1. Suggest several verses of Scripture that speak of God's will.
2. What do we mean in general by the phrase "the will of God"?
3. According to 2 Peter 3:9, what is God's will regarding the salvation of mankind?
4. What is God's will for each follower of Jesus Christ, according to 1 Thessalonians 4:3, 7?
5. Suggest eight helpful guidelines regarding understanding God's will.

NOTES

1. A. W. Tozer, "Four Ways to Find God's Will," *HIS Magazine*, May 1969, 9.

2. S. Maxwell Coder, *God's Will for Your Life* (Chicago: Moody, 1946), 97.

3. Alan Redpath, *Getting to Know the Will of God* (Chicago: InterVarsity, 1954), 14–15.

4. Paul Little, *Affirming the Will of God* (Downers Grove, Ill.: InterVarsity, 1971), 6.

5. F. B. Meyer, *The Secret of Guidance* (New York: Revell, 1896), 14.

6. G. Christian Weiss, *The Perfect Will of God* (Chicago: Moody, 1950), 15.

7. Marion H. Nelson, *How to Know God's Will* (Chicago: Moody, 1963), 39.

8. J. Sidlow Baxter, *Does God Still Guide?* (Grand Rapids: Zondervan, 1968), 33.

9. Coder, *God's Will for Your Life*, 97.

"With great power the apostles *continued* to
testify to the resurrection of the Lord Jesus,
and much grace was upon them all."

ACTS 4:33 (NIV, ITALICS ADDED)

"The early church had no Bibles, no seminaries,
no printing presses, no literature, no educational
institutions, no radio, no television, no automobiles,
no airplanes; and yet within one generation the
gospel had been spread to most of the known world.
The secret of the spread of this gospel
was the power of the Holy Spirit."

BILLY GRAHAM, *PEACE WITH GOD*

"But you shall receive power when the Holy Spirit
has come upon you; and you shall be witnesses
to Me in Jerusalem, and in all Judea and
Samaria, and to the end of the earth."

ACTS 1:8

"I have never found witnessing to come naturally and
easily. Some of you may find this difficult to believe,
but by nature I'm a shy, reserved person; initiating
conversations with strangers is sometimes difficult
for me. . . . I don't even know if evangelism is my
spiritual gift. What I do know is that God has made it
crystal clear in His word that every Christian is to
'go and make disciples in all nations.'"

BILL BRIGHT, *WITNESSING WITHOUT FEAR*

12

SHARING
THE GOOD NEWS

NO POWER KNOWN to man even remotely compares to the power of a holy life. In the New Testament book of Acts this power is illustrated time and again.

One of the first of those incidents occurred in chapters 3 and 4 of Acts. As chapter 3 begins, Peter and John are on their way to the temple at the hour of prayer. When they arrive, they are met at Solomon's porch by "a certain man lame from his mother's womb" (3:2). He asks them for alms, but they give him something incomparably better.

"Silver and gold I do not have," Peter says, "but what I do have I give you: In the name of Jesus Christ of Nazareth, rise up and walk" (v. 6). The beggar does just that, creating a gigantic stir.

A crowd gathers and Peter proclaims the gospel to

them. The man was healed by the resurrection power of Jesus, Peter says, and they need to come to Him for salvation: "Repent therefore and be converted, that your sins may be blotted out, so that times of refreshing may come from the presence of the Lord" (3:19).

By this time the religious authorities—including the Sadducees, who rejected all possibility of resurrection—are aware of the disturbance. They are "greatly disturbed" when they realize that Peter and John are teaching the people and preaching "in Jesus the resurrection from the dead" (4:1–2) and have the two apostles jailed.

Only a few weeks earlier, the council of religious leaders had condemned Jesus to death. Any talk of His resurrection and healing in His name traumatized them. However, the proof of a spectacular miracle that had taken place was so obvious that pandemonium had broken loose. A man who was lame for forty years was standing, walking, leaping, and praising God before their very eyes (Acts 3:8–9).

TWO COMMONERS
WITH COURAGE FOR GOD

Though commoners, Peter and John caused sheer panic in the hearts of the authorities, as the two apostles stood before the elite lawyers and theologians of the day.

What gave Peter and John courage in their witness? How was it, that two ordinary men, "uneducated and untrained," displayed greater influence than the best and brightest of their generation? The answer is, they were *holy men of God.* They were *steeped in Christ's Word* after following Him through three years of ministry. Their lives had been transformed by His resurrection.

They were *men of prayer.* They were *trusting in Him and obeying His commands.*

This level of life and dependence on God gave them the power they needed for effective witnessing. When the religious leaders "saw the boldness of Peter and John, and perceived that they were uneducated and untrained men, they marveled. And they realized that they had been with Jesus" (4:13).

OUR POWER FOR
AN EFFECTIVE WITNESS

The good news is that this power is available to the believer today, and it is the basis of all effective witnessing. No truly effective witness can take place unless the characteristics evident in Peter and John's lives—holy living, devoted to Christ's Word, people of prayer, trusting in Christ and obeying His commands— are present in the one who witnesses today.

The right motives energized the apostles that day in the temple. They had *knowledge* of the Lord Jesus and His salvation. They had been greatly *blessed* by the Lord Jesus as He worked in their lives. They had accepted the *Great Commission* recorded in the closing words of Matthew (28:19–20). As a consequence of all this, they had *position* in Christ that made them responsible to share the gospel as widely as they could.

OUR KNOWLEDGE
MAKES US RESPONSIBLE

I remember when Dr. Jonas Salk discovered the final phases of the polio vaccine. At last, there was a cure that would free millions of people from the fear of suffering from the crippling disease of polio. But just suppose Dr. Salk had decided to withhold that life-saving vaccine. Such a decision would be uncaring, if not criminal.

Likewise, each believer has the cure for the affliction of sin. We have the chance to make a lasting difference in the lives of others.

Writing to the congregation in Rome, Paul

explained his personal responsibility. "I am a debtor both to Greeks and to barbarians, both to wise and to unwise. So, as much as is in me, I am ready to preach the gospel to you who are in Rome also" (Romans 1:14–15). The weight of this debt drove Paul relentlessly for a lifetime.

The world doesn't owe any of us anything; however, we believers owe the world—we owe people a caring, intelligent presenting of "God's Good News." Simply put, to *know* is to *owe*. Our knowledge makes us responsible.

OUR BLESSINGS
MAKE US RESPONSIBLE

To possess God's salvation imposes responsibility. To *have* is to *owe*. The intriguing story in 2 Kings 7:3–11 of four starving lepers outside the gates of Samaria illustrates this truth. Their situation was desperate. The city was surrounded by an enemy army. As lepers, they were forbidden to enter the city, yet if they didn't get food they would die of starvation. They decided to throw themselves upon the mercy of the Syrian army. Upon entering the camp, however, they found it deserted!

The Scripture tells us why:

The Lord had caused the army of the Syrians to hear the noise of chariots and the noise of horses —the noise of a great army. . . . Therefore they arose and fled at twilight. . . . And when [the] lepers came to the outskirts of the camp, they went into one tent and ate and drank. . . . Then they said to one another, "We are not doing what is right. This day is a day of good news, and we remain silent." (vv. 6–9)

Once these four lepers had eaten, they were burdened with concern for those who were still starving. They confessed that they had good news and were obligated to share it with others.

This powerful truth applies to each person who possesses spiritual salvation and for one reason or another neglects to witness. It is sinful to be silent when we possess the good news. Our blessings make us responsible.

The Old Testament prophet Ezekiel writes about the issue of human responsibility:

When I say to the wicked, "O wicked man, you shall surely die!" and you do not speak to warn the wicked from his way, that wicked man shall die in his iniquity; but his blood I will require at your hand. Nevertheless if you warn the wicked to turn from his way, and he does not turn from his way, he shall die in his iniquity; but you have delivered your soul. (Ezekiel 33:8–9)

Ezekiel met his responsibility by speaking out. This passage teaches that failure to sound the warning incurs individual responsibility.

Jesus Himself taught responsibility in the story of the Good Samaritan in Luke 10:30–37. In this parable, a priest and a Levite both saw the desperate condition of a beaten traveler, yet they passed by and did nothing. Their sin was their failure to do something for the beaten man. Their blessings made them responsible.

In the parable of the talents (Matthew 25:14–30), the worker with one talent was condemned because he buried his talent and did nothing to use it. He was accused of being both wicked and lazy (v. 26). The parable emphasizes that our blessings make us responsible. *To have . . . is to owe!*

THE GREAT COMMISSION
MAKES US RESPONSIBLE

Before Jesus ascended to heaven, His disciples wanted to know when Christ would set up His kingdom. He replied, "It is not for you to know times or seasons which the Father has put in His own authority" (Acts 1:7). After telling them what they were *not* to know, He then outlined exactly what they *were* to know: "But you shall receive power when the Holy Spirit has come upon you; and you shall be witnesses to Me in Jerusalem, and in all Judea and Samaria, and to the end of the earth" (Acts 1:8). The commission of Jesus is so clear that no Christian can claim ignorance. Jesus stated, "You shall be My witnesses."

This was not the first time Jesus had given these instructions. All four Gospels end with a similar command (Matthew 28:18–20; Mark 16:15; Luke 24:46–49; John 20:21).

After reading Matthew 28:18–20, Pastor William Carey of England was deeply concerned for the people of India. He asked himself: Does this commission of Jesus apply to me? Does God really want me to go as His representative to share the good news? Carey decided to speak about this matter in a gathering of the local association of ministers. The presiding pastor bluntly rebuked young Carey and informed him that when God wanted to save the heathen, He would do it without his help. In spite of this rebuke, William Carey responded to the commission given by Jesus. He and his family accepted their responsibility to share the good news and became missionaries to India. William Carey is now known as the father of the modern missionary movement.

George Whitefield, challenged by the Great Commission, crossed the Atlantic Ocean thirteen times to reach the people of the American colonies. That was at a time when it took three months to cross the Atlantic in a sailing ship. Whitefield preached three and four times a day for thirty-three years. He had a specific burden for the people of the American colonies. He died at age fifty-five.

Much as God the Father sent Jesus into the world, God the Son is sending people today (John 20:21). Well, how *did* the Father send Jesus? He became one of us. The Word became flesh (John 1:14). And that is still God's approach. He uses ordinary people like you and me. The commission of Jesus . . . makes each believer responsible!

OUR POSITION
MAKES US RESPONSIBLE

The apostle Paul was sensitive regarding his position as a believer in Christ. He said, "We are ambassadors for Christ, as though God were pleading through us: we implore you on Christ's behalf, be reconciled to God" (2 Corinthians 5:20).

It is sobering to realize that Almighty God makes His appeal to people through you and me. Charles B. Williams, in his *New Testament in the Language of the People*, translates 2 Corinthians 5:20 powerfully: "So I am an envoy to represent Christ, because it is through me that God is making His appeal. As one representing Christ I beg you, be reconciled to God."

That awesome position implies responsibility. Each and every believer is either a good ambassador or a poor ambassador, but we cannot escape being an ambassador. In the light of our calling, we must share the good news.

Billy Graham has observed, "We Christians are now duly appointed and commissioned ambassadors of the King of kings. We are to let our flag fly high over our embassy. . . . If we are not willing to let our flags fly in the home, in the office, in the shop, on the campus—then we are not worthy to be ambassadors for Christ!"[1]

John Currier, a man who could not read or write, was found guilty of murder and sentenced to prison for life in 1949. Later he was transferred from prison and paroled to work for a wealthy farmer near Nashville, Tennessee.

In 1968, however, his sentence was terminated. State Correction Department records show that a letter was written to the convict and the farmer for whom he worked. The letter said he was free.

But Currier never saw the letter or even knew it had been written. One year went by, then two, then five, and finally, ten; and still he did not know that he was free.

By this time, the farmer to whom he had been paroled was dead, but Currier kept working, serving out his sentence on the farm. He received a little money each week for personal needs—five dollars at first, then a little more, and finally twenty dollars weekly.[2]

But life was hard and filled with labor. He slept in a drafty trailer, taking baths in a horse trough with a garden hose. Life held little joy and no promise.

This went on until 1978. Then a state parole officer

learned of his plight and told him of the missing letter. Carrier sued the State of Tennessee for $600,000. Some thought the sum was too small.

Would it matter to you if someone sent you an important message—the most important of your life—and year after year the urgent message was never delivered?

Think of a different situation. A child is born, grows up, and dies without once hearing that there is a God who loves him. He is never told that the God who made him sent His Son to deliver him from sin and give him everlasting life.

He lives in servitude to a cruel and powerful master, Satan. And his children are also born to live and die in bondage.

This is the condition of all those who live outside the circle of the family of God. Our position as an ambassador makes us responsible to witness.

REASONS TO PROCLAIM
THE GOOD NEWS OF JESUS

Why should you as a believer witness? Consider these four biblical reasons:

Our knowledge makes us responsible (Romans 1:14–17).

Our blessings make us responsible (2 Kings 7:3–9).

The Great Commission makes us responsible (Matthew 28:18–20).

Our position in Christ makes us responsible (2 Corinthians 5:20).

If that were not enough, consider the four motivations the apostle Paul mentions in 2 Corinthians 5.

1. The judgment of each believer awaits (v. 10).
2. The terror of the Lord awaits (v. 11).
3. The constraining love of Christ should compel us (v. 14).
4. The costly work of Christ should spur us to live for Him rather than for ourselves (v. 15).

Why should we witness? Because Jesus said so! That's reason enough!

THE CALL TO CONTINUE

Polycarp of Smyrna remains a great example of continuing the Christian life. A faithful church leader, Polycarp was martyred for his faith in AD 155.

The governmental authorities tried in every way to force him to renounce Jesus. The governor declared, "Curse Jesus and you will be set free."

"Eighty-six years I have served Jesus and He has done me no wrong," The old pastor answered. "How can I blaspheme my King who has saved me?" The flames then consumed him and he was burned alive. He was faithful unto death.[3]

So my challenge today is, Continue!

Continue!

And as you continue, rest in the apostle Paul's promise to believers (Philippians 1:6 NIV, italics added): "He who began a good work in you *will carry it on to completion* until the day of Christ Jesus."

QUESTIONS

1. What gave Peter and John the power and courage to witness in Acts 3 and 4?
2. Why does our knowledge of the gospel make us responsible to share the gospel?
3. What is our position before God according to 2 Corinthians 5:20, and why does that increase our responsibility?
4. List several facts from 2 Corinthians 5 that should motivate all believers in Christ to share the gospel.

NOTES

1. Billy Graham, *Peace with God* (Minneapolis: World Wide Publications, 1984), 173.

2. "Convict Was to Be Freed in 1968; He Says No One Told Him," *St. Petersburg Times*, February 6, 1979, sec. A, 1.

3. Paul L. Maier, *Eusebius: Church History* (Grand Rapids: Kregel, 1999), 145.

How to Begin the Christian Life

How to Begin the Christian Life is a modern classic. With more than 600,000 copies in print it has already helped tens of thousands begin their Christian lives. Now let it help you or someone you know. This little handbook will give you reliable scriptural guidance in these and other areas of Christian living.

978-0-8024-3582-8

How to Finish the Christian Life

Dr. George Sweeting's *How to Begin the Christian Life* revealed a plan for success in starting new lives of purpose in pursuit of Christ. Now he and his son, Donald Sweeting, present *How to Finish the Christian Life*, a guide that gives mature believers a new set of disciplines and encouraging truths to help them finish well.

978-0-8024-3588-0